Series/Number 07-087

ANALYTIC MAPPING AND GEOGRAPHIC DATABASES

G. DAVID GARSON
North Carolina State University

ROBERT S. BIGGS
Community Development and Planning
Wendell, North Carolina

SAGE Publications
International Educational and Professional Publisher
Newbury Park   London   New Delhi

For information address:

SAGE Publications, Inc.
2455 Teller Road
Newbury Park, California 91320
E-mail: order@sagepub.com

SAGE Publications Ltd.
6 Bonhill Street
London EC2A 4PU
United Kingdom

SAGE Publications India Pvt. Ltd.
M-32 Market
Greater Kailash I
New Delhi 110 048 India

Printed in the United States of America

Library of Congress Catalog Card No. 89-043409

Garson, G. David.
    Analytic mapping and geographic databases / G. David Garson, Robert S. Biggs.
        p.   cm.—(Quantitative applications in the social sciences; v. 87)
    Includes bibliographical references.
    ISBN 0-8039-4752-6
    1. Geographic informational systems. 2. Cartography—Data
processing. I. Biggs, Robert S. II. Title. III. Series: Sage
university papers series. Quantitative applications in the social sciences; 87.
G70.2.G37 1992   92-8652
526′.0285—dc20   CIP

97 98 99 00 01 02 8 7 6 5 4 3

Sage Production Editor: Judith L. Hunter

When citing a university paper, please use the proper form. Remember to cite the current Sage University Paper series title and include the paper number. One of the following formats can be adapted (depending on the style manual used):

(1) GARSON, G. D., & BIGGS, R. S. (1992) Analytic Mapping and Geographic Databases. Sage University Paper series on Quantitative Applications in the Social Sciences, 07-087. Newbury Park, CA: Sage.

OR

(2) Garson, G. D., & Biggs, R. S. (1992) *Analytic mapping and geographic databases* (Sage University Paper series on Quantitative Applications in the Social Sciences, series no. 07-087). Newbury Park, CA: Sage.

CONTENTS

SERIES EDITOR'S INTRODUCTION

In the social sciences, maps are neglected as an analytic tool. Given the influence of geography on human behavior, this neglect may seem hard to explain. Its roots appear to lie largely in the common difficulties of using maps effectively and efficiently. For example, suppose political scientist Jane White wishes to study the electoral geography of the Democratic vote in the 1988 U.S. presidential election. Does she prepare a choropleth map, shading in states (districts, counties?) according to percentage vote? If so, where does she get the map, which shades does she use, how accurate is the shading? When she looks at the finished map, does she see a relationship between, say, region of the country and vote? How does she quantify that relationship? Can other, nongeographic factors be incorporated into the examination of this relationship? What about the changes over time observed as similar maps are constructed from prior elections?

To answer all these questions, Professor White must somehow gather, store, present, and analyze these electoral geography data. Because such work has in the past involved intensive hand labor, it has been shunned by modern quantitative political scientists. Fortunately, this monograph by Garson and Biggs shows how these traditional difficulties can be overcome. The contemporary analyst has available a number of reasonably priced computer-based geographic information systems (GIS) packages, to which can be coupled any number of readily obtainable geographic data sources. For instance, the U.S. Bureau of the Census created TIGER (Topologically Integrated Geographic Encoding and Referencing) files, which contain the first digitized map of U.S. streets. TIGER can be joined to a GIS software package such as Safari (by Geographic Data Technology). After the researcher has selected the appropriate data set and software, he or she can turn directly to analytic mapping.

The authors review the many types of maps—UBC, dasymetric, block, isarithmic, to name a few—and explain myriad intriguing, seldom-seen summary statistics, such as geographic means, location quotients, and areal correspondence. Statistical appreciation leads to actual modeling with maps, where multivariate regression techniques may be pursued, as GIS software is interfaced with standard statistical packages such as SAS.

Potential applications of GIS and analytic mapping extend beyond the normal social science boundaries. Analytic mapping is already heavily used in government, as planners and policymakers work on problems of schools, rezoning, taxes, natural disasters, and crime. For instance, the Crime Analysis Mapping System in Tacoma, Washington, permits crime data to be mapped in sophisticated ways against census data. As Garson and Biggs make clear in this much-needed introduction, we can learn a great deal from this geography-driven alternative to conventional data analysis.

—*Michael S. Lewis-Beck*
Series Editor

ANALYTIC MAPPING AND GEOGRAPHIC DATABASES

G. DAVID GARSON
North Carolina State University

ROBERT S. BIGGS
Community Development and Planning, Wendell, North Carolina

1. INTRODUCTION

Analytic mapping using geographic databases is a field that has taken giant steps forward in the last decade. The last decade has been marked by (a) the "microcomputer revolution" and the availability of sophisticated geographic information systems (GIS) packages at the desktop level, affordable by most social scientists; (b) improved collection and dissemination of geographic data, including the U.S. Census Bureau's issuing the first digitized map of the entire United States; and (c) continued progress in the sophistication of analytic techniques applied by GIS software to geographic databases. Analytic mapping, like other visual approaches to data analysis, traditionally required unthinkable drudgery that now can be accomplished by computers. The full impact of this is quite recent. At the federal level, for instance, the number of agencies reporting widespread use of GIS is expected to more than double, from 18 in 1990 to 44 in 1992 (U.S. General Accounting Office, 1991). Analytic mapping has numerous applications, not only to government policy but also to a broad range of social science topics. The dynamic diffusion and distribution of any variable across area and over time falls within its purview. Only statistical analysis is more important for social scientists, yet it is a domain that seems to be avoided studiously in social graduate methods courses, the essential nature of which was formed in the era before analytic mapping techniques had become feasible for ordinary social scientists.

Unfortunately, GIS tends to become the province of organizational specialists rather than a generic tool, as happens with statistical packages. "Typically, an individual with some background in computing will hear of or see a geographical information system or automatic cartography system in operation and, by attending conferences or workshops, become a promoter," one analyst wrote recently. "With luck," the analyst continued, that person "will eventually assemble sufficient resources to acquire a system and can expect to be named manager of it. The rest of the agency will be very happy to know that the group is involved in the new technology, but equally happy to know that all obligation to understand it rests with the resident expert" (Tomlinson Associates, 1989, p. 174). Substitute a disciplinary reference to economics, political science, psychology, or sociology for "agency" in this description and one has a statement equally applicable to the social sciences.

A geographic information system is a constellation of hardware and software that integrates computer graphics with a relational database for the purpose of managing data about geographic locations (Ripple, 1989). These geographic data are both spatial and descriptive in nature. The descriptive data and text are stored in the relational database. The unique GIS component is a system that can track such spatial concepts as "nearness" of one database record relative to another, as well as other possible relations such as "north/south," "inside/outside," or "above/below." In advanced applications, relations may include orientation of geographic units vis-à-vis prevailing sun paths, prevailing wind paths, and noise patterns, or may involve three-dimensional mapping, as in the GIS for the cleanup of Boston Harbor (Ardalan, 1988).

Computer mapping is particularly important in government, and hence is salient to social scientists who study government policies. It has been estimated that 80% of the informational needs of local government policymakers are related to geographic location (Williams, 1987, p. 151). Rezoning actions are a common example, as are many activities associated with public works, tax appraisal, utility regulation, and planning. Computerization of mapping functions allows census, tax, crime, and other data to be projected onto maps; allows all maps to be updated in a centralized way not susceptible to map deterioration or loss; allows easy access to maps, including automatic output in any scale desired; and automatically provides map-related data (e.g., mailing labels for all property owners adjacent to any parcel affected by a rezoning hearing).

The U.S. Census Bureau's TIGER (Topologically Integrated Geographic Encoding and Referencing) system has revolutionized mapping, enabling incredibly detailed analysis. Geographic information systems are now a billion-dollar industry, partly because the graphical analyses that emerge from GIS are found by decision makers to be more useful than traditional statistical analyses that dominate the social sciences. Even in the area of statistical analyses, graphic representation of data arrays has emerged as a preferred modeling and exploration technique. Social science departments tend to abandon these increasingly important domains to computer scientists, geographers, and marketing specialists, but techniques from these domains deserve a central place in methodological instruction in the social sciences.

Geographic information systems are destined to play an ever-larger role in social science analysis. A uniform national policy on this was established by Revised Circular A-16, signed October 19, 1990, by U.S. Office of Management of Budget Director Richard Darman. The circular establishes the Federal Geographic Data Committee (FGDC), the purpose of which is to develop guidelines for a national digital spatial information resource, along with state and local governments and the private sector. Lowell Starr, director of the National Mapping Division of the U.S. Geological Survey, called the circular the "most significant event in the last decade to coordinate surveying, mapping, and related spatial data" (quoted in Warnecke, 1990, p. 45). Building on but not limited to the Census Bureau's TIGER database, discussed in a later section, this policy initiative embraces literally hundreds of millions of dollars of development, the fruits of which are relevant to a broad range of policy domains of interest to social scientists (see Bossler, Finnie, Petchenik, & Musselman, 1990). For a history of GIS and mapping, see Parent and Church (1989).

While large-scale GIS applications require the power of mainframe computing, much of the power of GIS may be applied to social science applications through the use of easily accessible microcomputers. This is especially true of 32-bit microcomputers such as those based on the 80386 chip, which is rapidly becoming the standard for academic computing in the 1990s. In this monograph we are concerned primarily with exactly this sort of application, not with specialized software used by professional geographers on mainframes, where, unlike in social science, there is a need to be cartographically correct to within a matter of feet or even inches.

Terminology

A geographic information system can be defined as a constellation of hardware and software that integrates computer graphics with a relational database for the purpose of managing data about geographic locations. Like all definitions, however, this one raises issues. *Managing data* is an ambiguous phrase: GIS generally also store, retrieve, analyze, overlay, display, and print maps and reports, though any given GIS software package may do more or less than this. Moreover, early GIS databases were not always relational, though this is nearly universal today.

GIS TERMS

Some GIS are used for legal purposes, such as tracking properties for purposes of tax assessment. These are called *cadastral* databases, since they deal with publicly recorded surveys and maps associated with ownership title to property. Cadastral databases are only one of many kinds of *geographic* databases, which may deal with any geocoded spatial information. *Geocoding* refers to the assignment of spatial identifiers to points, lines, or features, as by assignment of latitude/longitude coordinates to point data. *Parallel* is a synonym for latitude, and *meridian* is a synonym for longitude. Coordinates are measured with respect to the equator and the prime meridian (which runs through Greenwich, England) in degrees, minutes, and seconds. For instance, "100 28 40 W" is short for "100 degrees, 28 minutes, 40 seconds west of the prime meridian." If no direction is added, the default direction is assumed to be east of the prime meridian or north of the equator. *Scale* is the ratio of map distances to real distances, where "small-scale maps" are maps of large areas such as countries and "large-scale maps" are maps of smaller areas, such as neighborhoods. Block maps might be 1:2,000 in scale, for instance, and country maps might be 1:1,000,000. "RF 1:1,000,000" means "representative fraction" on a scale of 1 to 1,000,000. Often this ratio would mean 1 millimeter to 1 kilometer.

A map scale is the ratio between map distance and real distance, where the map distance is usually represented as 1. For instance, 1:100,000 means 1 map inch equals 100,000 real inches, which is about 1.6 miles. One of the advantages of vector mapping is that display to any scale can be done automatically, so that small features can be shown in greater scale than large features on different maps. A large-scale map is one with a smaller term in the denominator of the ratio. For instance, 1:10,000 maps are large scale compared with 1:1,000,000 maps.

Coordinates are normally those based on the North American Datum of 1983 (NAD83), but sometimes with older data one may find coordinates based on the North American Datum of 1927 (NAD27). The National Geodetic Survey's NADCOM program is the standard method for converting NAD27 coordinates to NAD83 coordinates. Commercial utilities such as Tralaine are also available for this purpose.

The distance between any two map points is not a straight line on a two-dimensional piece of paper. Rather, the shortest distance is along a *great arc* circle around the globe, such that the perimeter of the circle passes through the two points and the center of the circle is the center of the earth. The *azimuth* is the direction of a great arc circle, measured as an angle in degrees from north. When specifying a direction in a GIS, one is specifying an azimuth, though some systems allow users to enter compass points (E, ENE, NE, and so on).

Features are regions, lines, or points, where *regions* are areas such as tracts, political divisions, or user-defined regions, usually but not always contiguous in nature. Many GIS use the term *feature* to refer to areas together with the lines and points that they contain. Regions, lines, and points must all be geocoded. Regions are also called *areas* and *polygons*. Some regions include multiple polygons, such as interior lakes (Great Salt Lake) or exterior islands (the Florida Keys). These are called *lakes* and *islands* on the basis of being interior or exterior polygons, even if they are not, in fact, lakes or islands (e.g., Lesotho is a "lake" inside the Union of South Africa). Because alternative projections affect the relative size of features, choice of projection can bias the display. For instance, Mercator projections have been accused of being "Eurocentric" because of the size with which Europe is displayed (Rice, 1990).

Topology, which is the mathematics of spatial relationships, in a mapping context refers to the definition and management of points, lines, and areas in an integrated fashion such that changes in one element are adjusted for automatically in all related elements in the GIS. In particular, it is important in mapping that common borders be maintained so that "slivers" do not appear (small gaps or overlaps at boundary lines where regions meet). Better digitizing packages will allow the user to "clean" such areas of gap or overlap by detecting suspect areas and prompting the user to correct them. User-defined parameters can also be set whereby if gaps are detected by the program it will automatically correct them according to logical convention.

Features are organized into *layers* in a GIS. Various layers may contain political boundaries, census boundaries, roads, streams, or police station points. The coordinates for these are stored in region layer files, line layer files, or point layer files, depending on the nature of the contents. This form of organization allows map overlays to be turned on and off for different views of the data, and the intersections of different layers can be used to create new layers.

Generally in GIS features are mapped on a *vector* basis, which means that a file is maintained that defines a feature as the sequence of lines through a series of point coordinates. The vector approach links point coordinates into whole forms such as polygons to create map regions and curves that define individual map elements. Vector-based maps store geographic information as chains of x-y coordinates, used for drawing map images. The vector basis allows maps to be drawn in different scales, orientations, and layers without distortion. In addition to GIS software, commercial vector graphics packages such as Corel Draw, Applause II, Harvard Graphics, Freelance Plus, and Mirage can be used to manipulate vector files.

Alternatively, features can be mapped on a *raster* or *bitmap* basis, as through recording aerial photographs, just as any other image can be saved in computer files. The raster approach presents all map features simultaneously as elements in a grid and therefore lacks any relational structure. Raster image maps simply store a picture of a map as a series of pixels (points), just as one would a digitized photograph. Raster images can be edited by adjusting the colors of individual pixels (the smallest points displayable), but if images are shrunk or expanded too much, jagged edges and other distortions appear. Sheryaev (1977) and others have developed methods for standardizing and improving the efficiency of raster methods in cartography. Commercial graphics packages such as PC Paintbrush and Applause Paint support raster graphics. While raster images can be very detailed and colorful, they cannot be manipulated flexibly and play little role in most GIS systems. A process called *autotracing* converts raster into vector files.

Actual editing of vector or raster files may be accomplished within more powerful GIS packages, or may be accomplished through CAD (computer-aided design) software, which allows editing, overlaying, labeling, and other manipulation of images. CAD packages specifically tailored for mapping are sometimes called CAM (computer-aided mapping) or AM/FM (automated mapping/facilities management) packages. AM/FM offers a high level of precision in mapping functions and data management capabilities, but differs from GIS in its inability to locate points within a polygon and in its lack of presentation-quality map output.

PROJECTIONS

A *projection* is the method by which a spherical surface is translated into two-dimensional representation on a piece of paper (see Snyder & Steward, 1988). *Conformal* projections preserve local angles between features, which means that the shape of areas is preserved. That is, the angle between two intersecting lines is the same on a conformal map as it is on a globe. Conformal projections distort the shape of long features. The four most common conformal projections are the Mercator, the stereographic, the transverse Mercator, and the Lambert conformal conic.

There are numerous introductory texts on map projections (e.g., Dent, 1990, chap. 2; McDonnell, 1979; Monmonier, 1991, chap. 2; Richardson & Adler, 1972; Snyder, 1987). Nyerges and Jankowski (1989; Jankowski & Nyerges, 1989) have developed an expert system to help users determine which projection is appropriate to their research needs. In general, equidistant projections are best for general reference maps. Conformal projects are usually preferred for navigation, meteorology, military applications, and large-scale maps. Equal-area projections are used for statistical distribution maps (Maling, 1973). For educational use in illustrating projections, the World Projection and Mapping System is microcomputer software capable of displaying some 200 named map projections, allowing the user to set scale and rotation.

The Mercator projection is the oldest and most common, still used in navigation, but it renders Greenland the size of South America, whereas on a globe it is only an eighth as large. The transverse Mercator projection is widely used in topographical maps and as a base for the Universal Transverse Mercator (UTM) plane coordinate system. The Lambert conformal projection is especially appropriate where east-west (latitudinal) direction and shape are critical, as in air navigation charts. The stereographic projection produces a circular azimuthal map in which circles on the globe plot as circles on the map, useful in plotting radio wave ranges and the like.

Equal-area projections preserve the relative size of regions and are thus often used for instructional purposes and in small-scale maps (e.g., country maps). Equal-area maps cannot be conformal. The Albers equal area conic projection is appropriate for middle-latitude areas of greater east-west and lesser north-south extent. As such, it is used as a standard base map for the United States by the U.S. Census. Lambert's equal-area projection is also azimuthal (see below), hence producing a circular map, and is symmetrical with respect to distortion and is therefore useful where equal emphasis is placed on east-west and north-south dimensions around a focal point, as in continent maps. The cylindrical equal-area projection, using standard parallels of 30 degrees, produces a rectangular map with the least angular distortion of any equal-area map, though it "doesn't look right" to people used to Mercator and other common projections. The Mollweide projection, which produces an oval map, has least distortion in middle latitudes and is sometimes used to portray world population and other distributions. The sinusoidal equal-area projection creates an onion-shaped map such that parallels appear to be equally spaced, useful for emphasis on latitudinal relations and sometimes used for maps of South America. Goode's homolosine equal-area projection creates a composite map portrayed in six lobes based on sinusoidal projections in equatorial zones and Mollweide projections in high-latitude areas.

Equidistant projections preserve the scale and distance between one point on a map and all other points. For instance, azimuthal equidistant projections portray directions and distances from the center (but not from other map points) correctly, useful for any portrayal of radiation (radio waves, seismic events). Such maps have enormous shape distortions at the outer edge of the circular map.

Azimuthal projections produce circular maps that preserve the direction between all points in relation to a central point. If the map user focuses on a city or point other than the central point of the azimuthal map, directions from this other point will not be accurate. In azimuthal projections the globe is projected onto a plane made tangent to any point on the globe. Distortions are symmetrical around the center of the projection. The stereographic projection is conformal and azimuthal; Lambert's equal-area projection is equal area and azimuthal; and, of course, the azimuthal equidistant projection is equidistant and azimuthal. Gnomic projections are another type of azimuthal projection that portrays great circle arcs (the shortest path between two points on a globe) as straight lines, useful for marine navigation and the like.

There are many other projections, some combinations of the types just discussed. A noteworthy example is the Robinson projection, developed in 1961 for Rand McNally, to meet the objective of minimizing the appearance of area and angular distortion when portraying the world. Another is the space-oblique Mercator projection, which is not quite a conformal projection. This projection is used by LANDSAT orbiting satellites, where the curved groundtrack of the satellite is used as the central line of projection.

Utility software such as Tralaine is available to convert data from one projection to another, and many GIS packages themselves contain some built-in projection conversion ability. (Contact information about Tralaine and other software mentioned in this volume may be found in the Appendix.)

Social scientists should be aware that in a joint resolution, seven major professional organizations have condemned use of the Mercator and other (Gall, Gall-Peters, Miller) projections that use a rectangular map in which longitudes and latitudes are parallel lines. This traditional projection, developed in the sixteenth century, seriously distorts the relative size of continents (or, in the case of Gall-Peters, the shape). The Mercator projection shows

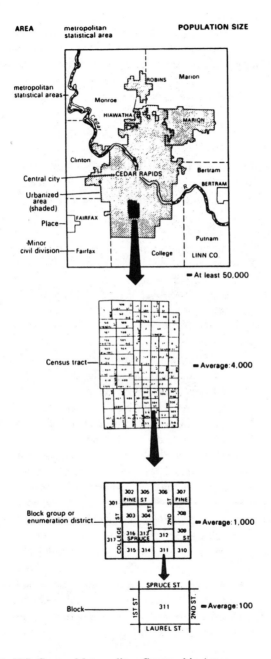

Figure 1.1. U.S. Census Metropolitan Geographic Areas
SOURCE: U.S. Bureau of the Census (1979, p. 4).

areas disproportionately larger as one approaches either pole. The National Geographic Society (NGS) has adopted the Robinson projection in place of the Mercator. Other societies joining the NGS in this 1989 resolution were the American Cartographic Association, the Association of American Geographers, the Canadian Cartographic Association, the National Council for Geographic Education, and the Special Libraries Association (Geography and Map Division).

CENSUS TERMS

Census areas are of two types: political and statistical areas. On the political side, note that some data tables include not only the 50 U.S. states but also the District of Columbia, Puerto Rico, and outlying areas (Virgin Islands, Guam, American Samoa, the Northern Mariana Islands, and Palau) as statistical equivalents to states. A *county* is a first-order division of a state and includes parishes in Louisiana, boroughs and census areas in Alaska, *municipios* in Puerto Rico, and independent cities in several states (Maryland, Missouri, Nevada, Virginia). Also included as a county is Yellowstone National Park in Montana. A *minor civil division* (MCD) is a legally defined subcounty area; in 1990, only 28 states had MCDs, plus barrios in Puerto Rico. A *sub-MCD* is a legally defined subdivision of a subcounty area (subbarrios in Puerto Rico).

Continuing the distinctions among political areas in the census, an *incorporated place* is a political unit that is incorporated as a city, town, borough, or village, not counting towns in New England, New York, and Wisconsin, and not counting boroughs in Alaska and New York. A *voting district* (VTD) is any of several types of areas, including election districts, precincts, legislative districts, and wards as defined by state and local governments. (The 1980 census used the term "election precinct" instead of "voting district.") Other political areas in the census include American Indian reservations and Alaska Native regional corporations (ANRCs).

Statistical areas in the census include the *census block*, which is a small area bounded by streets or prominent physical features (see Figure 1.1). Blocks never cross block numbering area, census tract, or county boundaries. Each block receives a three-digit code number with a possible single letter suffix. There are about 7 million blocks in the United States. A *block group* is a combination of census blocks that share the same first digit in their codes. There are 230,000 block groups in the 1990 census. *Block numbering areas* (BNAs) are areas cooperatively defined by a state and the Census Bureau for grouping blocks in areas where census tracts are not established. There are 11,500 BNAs in the 1990 census, none of which cross county lines. *Census tracts* are small, locally delineated areas within selected counties, established by local committees and originally designed to have homogeneous demographic attributes. There were 50,400 census tracts in the 1990 census.

A *census designated place* (CDP) is a densely populated center lacking legally defined corporate limits or powers. CDPs are defined by the Census Bureau in cooperation with state officials and local data users. There were 5,300 CDPs in the 1990 census. *Unorganized territories* (UTs) are areas designated by the Census Bureau for areas where no minor civil division (MCD) exists in a state that has MCDs. There were 282 UTs in the 1990 census. A *census county division* (CCD) is an area designated by the Census Bureau in cooperation with state and local officials in states that do not have MCDs or that have MCDs that are not adequate for statistical reporting. There were 5,581 CCDs in the 1990 census. Other statistical areas include tribal jurisdiction statistical areas (TJSAs), tribal designated statistical areas (TDSAs), and Alaska Native village statistical areas (ANVSAs).

Selected Examples of Analytic Mapping and Geographic Databases in the Social and Policy Sciences

Analytic cartography is a recognized division within the field of surveying and mapping (Moellering, 1991a). Developed by W. R. Tobler (1961) and William Bunge (1962) in the 1960s, this perspective on mapping is marked by a heavy overlap between cartography and GIS (Moellering, 1991b, p. 8). Computerization has been essential to the growth of analytic cartography, allowing a focus on manipulation of "virtual maps" in electronic form rather than just "real maps" on paper sheets. As Nyerges (1991) has observed, however, "We are still using virtual maps primarily for locational-level questions, and only approaching the distribution and pattern-level questions at a rudimentary level in analytical systems, particularly in GIS" (p. 13). For instance, few GIS packages adequately handle temporal change of boundaries or display of temporal change of values in given boundaries (for an exception, see Langran, 1990).

That is, analytic mapping is still a young field and some of its potential uses of most interest to social scientists are not yet well developed. Present GIS systems are very good at answering questions such as, Where is the phenomenon of interest? but may not lend themselves as well to answering questions of the type, How has the phenomenon changed over time and what factors have influenced this? There is a need to alter present GIS packages to incorporate data models more consonant with analytic purposes. While the need for teamwork between social scientists and cartographers is well recognized by the latter group (see Nyerges, 1991, p. 20), GIS is still a largely unrecognized opportunity in the social science community.

In spite of limitations, analytic mapping and GIS constitute a rapidly expanding field. Spatial decision support systems are a research initiative of the National Center for Geographic Information and Analysis (Densham & Goodchild, 1989), for instance. At a level of more immediate application, GIS is a major MIS specialization and is the leading focus of URISA (the Urban and Regional Information Systems Association), the professional association for public sector MIS officials concerned with state and local information systems applications. URISA sponsors an annual GIS/LIS conference in conjunction with other interested organizations such as the American Planning Association, the American Public Works Association, and the Association of American Geographers. GIS applications include producing near real-time battlefield mapping during the 1991 Gulf War (Green, 1991); tracking earthquake fault lines in relation to property data for loss-risk assessment in Utah (Firestone, 1987); flood hazard mapping in Washington, D.C. (Cotter & Campbell, 1987); emergency preparedness functions in Los Angeles regarding evacuation routing, shelter allocation, and identification of probable disaster locations (Johnson, 1987); and helping Portsmouth, New Hampshire, preserve its supply of clean water (Lee & Douglass, 1988).

The utility of graphic presentation of map data is illustrated in the Crime Analysis Mapping System (CAMS) of the City of Tacoma, Washington. CAMS allows police and other users to view data on burglaries, rape, and other crimes in conjunction with census data. Data may be viewed at street, arterial street, census block, district, and subdistrict levels. Using a tablet-type data entry screen, police can select the level of analysis, type of crime, and filter conditions (e.g., dates), then view the pattern of crime dispersion. If desired, case numbers can be displayed to link map points to actual crime records. Systems such as CAMS can provide a clearer basis for analysis of such management decisions as assigning police patrols, interpreting case patterns, targeting education efforts, and planning facilities such as lighting. Microcomputer packages such as MapInfo are now used in most police departments to automate the process of producing maps of police jurisdictions with "pin" information on crime occurrence (Robb, 1990, p. 15). RealTime MapInfo can even link to satellite technology to track police cars and map their movement on maps that change in real time (Schroeder, 1991).

Many software packages have been developed specifically for planning purposes, often public sector in nature, and these lend themselves to many social science applications as well. Examples include FMS/AC, MunMAP, and Plantech. For a review of literature on computers and planning, see Klosterman (1988, 1990).

DISTRIBUTIVE ANALYSIS

The basic form of analysis in mapping is display of the distribution of some attribute across map features. Distributive mapping is used in conjunction with conventional statistical tabulation of attributes by map feature, with colors, hatching patterns, symbol sizes, or other design features indicating the statistical range of each feature. For instance, Weisburd, Maher, and Sherman (1989) used computer mapping on police call-for-service data to investigate alternative theories of criminality, using the distribution and clustering of types of crime as evidence. Similar mapping analyses have been undertaken by the Chicago Police Department, the University of Illinois at Chicago, and Northwestern University using MAPADS (micro-computer-assisted police analysis and deployment system; see Maltz, Gordon, & Friedman, 1991). In a second example, Fitts (1989) used computer maps to analyze the distribution of linguistic patterns among Alabama blacks based on survey research concerning responses to lexical items in the *Linguistic Atlas of the Gulf States*. As a third instance, Hillier (1989) has used computer-generated map data to analyze the growth patterns in English and French villages and towns, comparing settlement growth patterns to organic growth simulations. For a fourth example, a Northwestern University team helps activist community groups by providing computerized maps showing where the city government is expending its budget (McCullough, 1991, p. 14).

SPATIAL PROXIMITY ANALYSIS

Another simple use of GIS is proximity analysis. This class of problems centers on finding the map features that correlate with a given dependent variable. Spatial analysis is used routinely for site selection problems, environmental impact analysis, diffusion and epidemiological studies, and problems of geographic correlation. For instance, it has been hypothesized that electromagnetic fields may be harmful medically. Joseph Bowman (Department of Preventative Medicine, University of Southern California) used FMS/AC to correlate child leukemia, magnetic field measurements for more than 350 homes, and characteristics and locations of electric utility devices and circuits within a 200-foot radius. The circuits and devices in and surrounding each home are mapped on FMS/AC, which can also compute distances.

DIFFUSION ANALYSIS

Diffusion analysis is simply spatial proximity analysis tracked over time. A sequence of distribution maps taken at periodic intervals provides a clear picture of diffusion, and today such images can be animated using slide show modules that are part of most graphics packages (e.g., PC-Key-Draw). In the early 1950s, Hägerstrand (1968) pioneered the Monte Carlo simulation method for modeling such diffusion patterns. The Monte Carlo method generates data that simulate diffusion, and the modeling process can add resistance factors or blocks between individuals or areas. The researcher can adjust these factors to simulate an observed pattern of diffusion for a set of test periods, then validate the model using a different set of time periods. In economics, spatial structure analysis centers on modeling the correlates of the geographic distribution of production facilities and other economic variables. As the models are dynamic, spatial diffusion or agglomeration over time is studied in particular. For instance, Beckmann and Puu (1985, 1990) have shown how in the distribution of production activities, local resource availability declines as a factor. At the same time, falling transportation costs, interregional trade, and improving technology transform constant-returns-to-scale activities (which favor diffuse spatial structure) into increasing returns-to-scale activities (which favors agglomeration). For a discussion of geographical models of urban growth in relation to transportation, see Selkirk (1982, chap. 14). For a discussion of random walks, Markov chains, and stochastic processes as applied to diffusion and related geographical analyses, see Wilson and Kirkby (1980, chap. 8) and Mather (1991, pp. 184-190).

RELATIVE SUITABILITY ANALYSIS

Relative suitability analysis is a variant of spatial analysis in which decision-making software is combined with the GIS to produce a composite choropleth map. Often used in site selection, packages such as the Land Use Planning template of FMS/AC support this form of analysis by allowing users to assign ranking weights to various conditions present in topologically structured polygon overlays. One may weight "median family income category" as 7 and weight "median education" as 4, for instance. The GIS will then produce a color-coded map in which colors indicate suitability by the criteria and weights assigned by the user. That is, a relative suitability map shows the pattern of polygons with the highest to lowest composite weighted score, displayed as a range of colors, hatch patterns, or scaled three-dimensional polygon models in which the most suitable areas are the tallest. GEODEX (Chandra & Goran, 1986) is an expert system for site suitability analysis, automating the process of applying land-use planning rules to given data and constraints.

SPATIAL DECISION SUPPORT

Spatial decision support addresses the issues of how many regions are needed to provide optimal service for geographically dispersed demand and where in each region its service center should be located (Densham & Rushton, 1988). A spatial decision support system (SDSS) is partly based on mathematical modeling, but it also must have a semistructured component that allows decision makers to inspect the results of mathematical models, then adjust them for factors that cannot be quantified as elements in an optimization algorithm. As noted by Armstrong, Densham, and Rushton (1986), SDSS contains a database, spatial data processing models, and a user interface for displaying maps and summary reports. A working SDSS is described by Armstrong et al. (1991) and applied to the problem of geographical reorganization of Iowa's area education agencies.

The spatial decision support system described by Armstrong et al. (1991) first requires the analyst to identify demand nodes (locations where there is a service demand), the weight of each demand node (how much demand at each location), and the locations of candidate service centers. It then uses Dijkstra's (1959) algorithm for creating a data set of the minimum weighted distances for each demand node to each candidate location that might serve it. This data set then becomes the input for location allocation software in the next stage. SDSS software next solves the p-median problem, which is the heart of optimization. A number of optimization functions are possible. Three supported by Armstrong's SDSS software are (a) finding p locations and their service areas such that average travel distance is minimized subject to a maximum distance constraint, (b) finding p locations such that a maximum amount of demand is within distance s of its closest location, and (c) finding the minimum number of locations keeping all demand within a specified distance s or its closest service location. Note that distance may be measured by route length, travel time, transportation cost, or some combination of these. Unique to the Armstrong software, SDSS can then analyze demand deficits, which are situations in which a given service location has less than a specified minimum demand or, in the case of equalization constraints, is more than a given percentage below the mean demand of all service locations. Whereas most GIS software addresses deficit adjustment by swapping small areas between contiguous districts, Armstrong's software uses a heuristic algorithm to reassign demand, which minimizes the increase in distances in the system.

Spider maps are a particular display format associated with spatial decision support systems, useful for showing the relationship of service centers to demand nodes. Spider maps are conventional boundary maps showing the area considered and the internal regional boundaries (e.g., service districts) that subdivide it. The locations of service centers are shown as dots within the regions. The "spider" takes the form of rays emanating from each dot (service center) to the location of each demand node served by the center. Optionally, one may use shading to indicate districts for demand nodes that are not served by their nearest service center. This occurs, of course, due to reassignment of some nodes during deficit adjustment (see above).

REDISTRICTING

Redistricting is illustrative of a class of analytic problems in which the user attempts to redraw boundary lines to optimize one or more goals while operating under a set of constraints. Redistricting problems are a particular case of a larger group of problems having to do with finding optimal ways of distributing objects of varying values into a given number of sets in such a way that the sets are of almost equal value and are as close to each other as possible. The Equalizer program written by mathematician James T. Parr (Illinois State University) accomplishes this, for instance (Wildgen, 1989). However, when the number of sets (e.g., voting districts) becomes large, a mathematical solution may exceed computer capacity and require a less precise but more efficient algorithmic approach, which is what is done using specialized redistricting software.

An example of such software is FMS/CENSUS, a module of the FMS/AC mapping systems, which in turn is based on the popular AutoCAD computer-assisted design package (see Omura, 1989; Thomas, 1989). FMS/CENSUS supports drawing and geocoding district boundaries (or importing them from other GIS packages); transforming these boundaries into topologically structured spatial database overlays; intersecting up to 12 political district boundaries with census block, tract, and voting district boundaries to establish a composite polygon overlay; correlating districts with a database containing 1990 census information; and redrawing boundaries to reassign census blocks to alternative districts, with changes reflected automatically in the database. An accompanying report feature aggregates census block records into summary tables defining the population counts for each existing or proposed political jurisdiction. In some cases, similar but simpler redistricting analyses can also prove fruitful using low-end mapping packages such as Atlas*Graphics (*GeoForum,* 1991).

NETWORK ANALYSIS

Network analysis addresses a class of problems in which the object is to analyze capacity and demand issues by simulating operational changes caused by opening and closing switches on the network. Water and utilities distribution are common fields of application of network analysis, but this technique can be applied to the flow of communications or the flow of people as well. FMS/AC software, for instance, supports network analysis, allowing the user to work inside a GIS map interactively to turn switch points on or off, logically connect network features, and trace network branches. The records that pertain to any given network trace can be isolated and their attributes examined.

SERIATION

Seriation is a classification procedure that has been used in archaeology, linguistics, geography, and other disciplines. The object of seriation is to order a series of objects (e.g., archaeological sites) by multiple criteria. Seriation can be as simple as the ordering of sites by frequency of occurrence of certain types of pottery (Larson & Michaelsen, 1990). However, the literature on mathematical seriation is extensive. Permutation search techniques (Hole & Shaw, 1967) and multidimensional scaling, cluster analysis, and similarity matrix methodologies have been used (Gelfand, 1969, 1971). Useful for generalizing about categorical and noncategorical map data, seriation had been limited by the labor-intensiveness of manual methods of rearranging geographical units by trial and error to find geographic sets characterized by similar attributes. Moreover, authorities disagreed on criteria by which to judge successful seriations. In recent years, however, objective criteria for seriation have been proposed and automated seriation procedures developed (Miller & Honsaker, 1983). Anthropologists such as Witschey (1989) have used computerized maps of ancient structures in conjunction with specialized computer programs (PROLOG based) to build seriation models. A seriation model arranges mapped structures into an ordered typology. By comparing the computer-derived seriation model for a new set of data with established typologies for related known objects or structures, inferences may be made about the nature and cultural history of the newly found objects or structures.[1]

2. GEOGRAPHIC DATABASES

Geographic Information Systems

Geographic information systems vary considerably in their scope and manner of organization. GIS can keep the same sort of data as do other computerized database managers, but they link it to features on one or more maps. When information is changed in the database (sometimes called a *geobase*), information displayed on the map(s) also changes. Nonetheless, GIS are usually designed to interface closely with conventional databases. MapInfo, for instance, can be used for a variety of built-in relational database analyses, including performance of complex SQL queries and calculations. (SQL, the structured query language, is the relatively new standard for exchange among different brands of database managers.) To take another example, the National Oceanic and Atmospheric Administration uses Arc/Info, a leading commercial database manager, integrated with its GeoCoast GIS.

Not all GIS packages can handle all problems. GIS intended for handling the data and mapping functions of a large city, for example, require packages capable of handling very large files, such as FMS/AC. Orlando, Florida, uses GIS/AMS software from GeoVision, Inc. (Darling, 1991). Often selection of large-scale GIS software is closely related to the choice of a database management system (DBMS) to be used throughout an organization or jurisdiction. Orlando chose GIS/AMS, for instance, because of its close connection to the Oracle DBMS. This connection allowed use of Oracle DBMS tools such as SQL*Forms and SQL*Reportwriter to manipulate attribute tables used by the GIS.

In general, GIS are organized around four types of information, which are organized in four types of files: geographic, map, attribute, and datapoint files. The file structure of various GIS vary considerably, but what follows is a composite overview of vector image mapping.

GEOGRAPHIC FILES

Geographic files are the core of geographic information systems. They contain information on features to be mapped. Features are the areas of interest, such as census tracts, counties, and school districts. For each feature, the geographic database will contain the x-y coordinates that define the feature. Typically, geographic files are boundary files, detailing the coordinates bounding counties, census tracts, school districts, or even offices within a building. Some boundaries are complex; for instance, Florida contains many islands in addition to its mainland.

A geographic file may also contain more than one layer (e.g., blocks and tracts and areas and states and countries), in which case there may be a layer settings file containing descriptive information about each layer (some GIS group the layer settings file as part of the map file, discussed next). Orange County, Florida, for instance, uses a right-of-way layer of street inventories, a flood plain layer, a zoning layer, a utilities layer, cadastral parcel (property ownership) layer, and a geodetics (survey and land record) layer in its GIS/AMS system. To take a second example, Atlas*GIS supports up to 250 map layers. There may also be line file overlays, containing coordinates of interior objects such as roads, railways, power lines, and rivers. Likewise, there may be point file overlays containing the coordinates of city centers, ZIP code centroids, postal code centers, and so on. Different GIS may store a limited amount of attribute data in the geographic files. Atlas*GIS, for instance, stores primary and secondary names, address ranges, and system-calculated areas, perimeter lengths, and centroids in four files it calls collectively "the geographic file."

MAP FILES

Map files, not to be confused with geographic files, usually contain information about the names of the geographic and other files that make up the geographic information system; data on labels, layers, and other layout aspects of the map, including file names used; program settings such as label and layer settings; and annotations added by the user, to be incorporated at printout time. Some GIS packages call these image files. The map file may contain names pointing to further files for this purpose, such as page layout files (color, scale, and other data for printouts of features and lines) and view files containing the coordinates for map borders.

ATTRIBUTE FILES

Attribute files are the type of data files social scientists are accustomed to using. They are rectangular data files of the ordinary sort, in which columns correspond to variables and rows correspond to cases. For geographic information systems, the cases are the features (areas) defined in the geographic file. That is, each row in the attribute file contains data on a single feature. Depending on the GIS, there may be logical and date fields within the attribute file as well as character and numeric fields.

Ordinary data files, such as .DBF files in dBASE format, can be the basis for attribute files, but an ID field must be added if not already present. Atlas*GIS, for instance, supports dBASE files, as do many others. The ID field contains the feature ID number from the geographic file corresponding to that record in the attribute file. The process of linking attribute information (or datapoint information, discussed below) to the geographic files is sometimes called *geocoding*.

Because the ID field is often a code with little if any meaning to the user, attribute files usually contain a field that is considered the primary name field. For a database of addresses, this could be people's names. A secondary name field is sometimes used as well to clarify possible ties on the primary field.

The GIS usually will create an attribute index automatically, ordering the attributes according to their feature IDs from the geographic file. There may also be an attribute field setting file containing the labels (names), descriptions, and structure information (if data are numeric or character, for instance) data on each attribute.

Attribute files often contain address information. Typically a street address is divided into five components: the number (e.g., 1234), the prefix direction (e.g., East), the name (e.g., Main), the street type (e.g., "Street"), and the suffix direction (e.g., "NW"). For GIS with address-matching capabilities, the attribute file with street information will also contain the start and stop points of the address range, usually each for the right and left sides of the street.

DATAPOINT FILES

Datapoint files contain information on particular points within features. Usually the coordinates for these points are kept in a point file associated with geographic boundary files, while other information about these points is kept in datapoint files. For instance, points might be municipalities where the geographic file is based on counties as features, and the datapoint file might contain economic, demographic, political, and other information on the municipalities. In datapoint files, columns are variables and rows are points defined by the point file.

Datapoint files are the same as other rectangular data matrices commonly used by social scientists, except that they must contain the ID of the corresponding record in the point file. In some GIS packages, the latitude and longitude of the points are kept in the datapoint file itself, with no point file. Usually the user must enter the coordinates of all desired points, but some packages, such as Atlas*GIS, can use TIGER files to match addresses supplied by the user and insert coordinates into a datapoint file automatically.

The geographic information system will usually create a datapoint index file to go with the datapoint file, in which datapoints are ordered by feature ID. This allows the GIS to locate quickly all datapoints associated with a feature of interest. The GIS may also create a datapoint field settings file that contains the labels (names) for all points, descriptions, and structure information.

OTHER FILES

In addition to geographic, map, attribute, and datapoint files, a GIS may have many other associated special-purpose files. For instance, there may be a color palette file that contains the master color list for each output device (on color selection, see Brewer, 1989; Robinson, Sale, Morrison, & Muehrcke, 1984, chap. 8). There may be a freehand file that holds data on the location and graphic attributes of any freehand objects to be placed on the map. There may be select files that contain lists of filtered feature, line, or datapoint IDs that have been preselected for analysis. The exact file structure of every GIS is different.

GIS SOFTWARE

Most GIS software centers user selections on "control panels," "menu bars," "status lines," and other methods of displaying information concisely. Often there is a menu bar or menu area at the top or left side of the screen. Highlighting such main menu bar choices as "File" often causes a submenu to pop up (e.g., load, rename, save, delete files). Submenu choices may lead to further pop-up menus or to a pick list (e.g., a list of files from which to choose) or to a fill-in form (e.g., a display title form, to specify text, font, size, color, and other settings for map titles). In some cases, such as a data entry choice on a menu, the user may be presented with a pop-up spreadsheet for entering row and column information. A large area in the middle of the screen is usually the work area where the map is actually constructed. A status line at the bottom or right side of the screen may contain information about default and user settings and current selections. Others use a command mode. For a checklist of selection criteria for choosing a particular GIS package, see Stefanovic and Drummond (1989).

The general nature of GIS is illustrated by considering the components of the status line in a particular package, Atlas*GIS. This is one of the leading microcomputer packages, used, for instance, by the Veterans Affairs Department to plan health facility use and construction (Taft, 1991). In this GIS, the status line can contain 15 bits of information:

1. the name of the currently active geographic file
2. the name of the currently active attribute file
3. the name of the currently active datapoint file
4. the name of the last map file loaded
5. the type of coordinate system in current use for projection purposes
6. the number of geographic features currently selected
7. the number of attribute fields currently selected
8. the number of datapoints currently selected
9. the current longitude of the cursor
10. the current latitude of the cursor
11. the current scale of the map
12. the current display mode (fast draft or slow final version)
13. the current input device (keyboard, mouse, tablet)
14. the tablet status (used in digitizing maps)
15. the redraw status (tells if the screen needs updating)

The general process in GIS use is to construct a map in the work area in the middle of the screen using various options from the menu area. As these choices are made, the status bar helps the user keep track of the process. Main menu choices in Atlas*GIS, for instance, are File (load and save), View (zoom in, pan), Select (select features; queries), Edit (view and/or modify features, layers, attributes, datapoints; browse files), Operate (analyses, address matching), Thematic (create choropleth maps), Display (set layers, labels, page size, scale, and other design features of the map), Print (hardcopy), Configure (program and device setup), and Help (online information).

While construction of a map can be accomplished with keyboard commands, the graphic nature of mapping makes use of a mouse or tablet the preferred input method. With most GIS the user can switch freely among all three devices. In general, graphics tablets are used for digitizing maps, a step not needed if one is planning to rely on "canned" boundary file products that are readily available for ZIP code areas, counties, and many other areas. A mouse is commonly used for pointing to screen locations, whether map coordinates or menu selections.

Users must be careful in opening maps that they save only what they want. Therefore, most GIS allow the user to open maps for read-only status, which allows viewing, printing, and querying, but not editing or saving. Alternatively, the user may be able to open maps on a "use-as" basis. This means the map is copied to a user-designated name, and changes made by the user are to the copy, not the original.

Image Processing. While most GIS packages store spatial information in terms of coordinates and vectors, cartographers sometimes need to deal with images directly, as in the case of aerial photographs. The process of dealing with images scanned into a computer is called *raster image processing.* Some GIS packages are integrated raster-vector systems and can handle both kinds of mapping data. A low-cost example is IDRISI, developed at Clark University and named after a famous medieval Islamic cartographer. Raster image processing functions illustrated by IDRISI include region building by grouping contiguous pixels (the smallest points displayed on a computer monitor); computation of distance, area, and perimeters of categorical coverages; analysis of slope and aspect; and image overlaying.

Software Selection. GIS packages span a broad price range, representative of the myriad features available. Selection of a package should be based on a detailed analysis of mapping and geobased data management needs. For some potential GIS users, the low-end "thematic mapping" packages will be adequate. These packages, such as Atlas*Graphics, offer a selection of common boundary files and solid map and data import functions. Such packages have the benefits of low cost, ease of use, and impressive map drawing and annotation features. However, the lack of precision to scale in map generation and the absence of map and data overlaying will eliminate such packages from consideration of those seeking higher-level GIS functionality.

As a basic feature, a GIS must be able to offer continuous mapping. The map base should not appear as separate panels but should be interconnected to provide analysis of contiguous parcels (regions) that appeared split on separate source data map sheets.

A most important consideration in GIS software selection will relate to the expected source of the map database. Many vendors of the more common packages will also offer a good selection of boundary maps. The importation of existing map bases is also an option. If TIGER or GBF/DIME (Geographic Base File/Dual Independent Map Encoding) files are a potential source of data, any package under consideration should offer import utilities necessary to facilitate the task. The other alternative in map generation is to build the database manually by digitizing source maps, discussed later. Most higher-end GIS packages offer digitizing utilities.

From a functionality perspective, features such as buffering, address matching, polygon overlaying, distance calculation, and data format should be considered. Many packages are designed for specific applications and, if appropriate, may make the selection process simple.

Data Reconciliation
Across Different Geographic Bases

It is common to find that data of interest are aggregated on different geographic bases. Not only may data exist at different levels of aggregation (city, county, state), but the boundaries of one basis may not correspond to those of another (fire districts may not correspond with census boundaries). Boundaries on one basis may overlap with boundaries on another basis, and in some cases boundaries on one basis may fail to cover some areas within boundaries on another basis. On top of all this, the temporal aspects (date of data collection) may be inconsistent across geographic databases. Changing map scales and merging data can easily lead to inaccuracy in spatial databases (Goodchild & Gopal, 1989). How are such problems to be handled?

RECONCILING POINT DATABASES

The simplest case arises when one has two databases, each of which represents points. Armstrong (1990), for instance, presents the case of reconciling information from the U.S. Geological Survey's WATSTORE database of raw water observations with the U.S. Environmental Protection Agency's MSIS database of finished water observations. Both contain data on wells as points but one lists by county and the other by county code; one lists by year/month, the other by date; one lists by a concatenated latitude/longitude code, the other by an ID number that can be linked to latitude and longitude. In such cases it is necessary to create look-up tables that show the correspondence of one way of coding (e.g., county names) to another (e.g., county codes). Either a conversion program must be created to translate the two data files into a single integrated database or the GIS software program must do the correspondence on the fly, using look-up tables in the course of analysis.

RECONCILING AREAS THROUGH AGGREGATION

Most GIS packages can handle data reconciliation through aggregation. For instance, client data gathered at the ZIP code level can be aggregated to the county level automatically. Better programs, such as Atlas*GIS, also handle the case of incompatible areas. For instance, if a lower layer such as a ZIP code area bridges two or more higher areas such as counties, the package can allocate the attribute on the basis of the percentage of the land area of the lower area in each of the higher areas. Both union (combining multiple regions with common or overlapping borders) and splitting (dividing one region by the intersections formed by the overlapping boundaries of another region) are supported by Atlas*GIS, as is area-weighted data aggregation (useful, for instance, in redistricting where a percentage of a region is to be transferred to a new layer).

RECONCILING AREAS THROUGH THE COMPATIBLE SURFACES METHOD

The Symap mapping package (Mather, 1991, chap. 4) of the Harvard Center for Environmental Design employed a local interpolation program that is more effective than the previous two approaches (Matson, 1985; Shepard, 1968). This approach, called the *compatible surfaces method*, is implemented in a few mapping packages, including PC Datagraphics and Mapping (PCDM; on its use with this package, see Hinze, 1989). The compatible surfaces method assumes that the control points on the surface with more areas are usable as a sample of the statistical density function for the surface with fewer areas.[2] In reconciling census block data with voting precinct data, for instance, the census surface has more areas and therefore data would be reconciled from the census block map to the voting precinct map. (Reconciling from larger areas to smaller ones can result in gross errors of estimate by this procedure.) In using the compatible surface method, it is also important that the population center, not the geographic center, be used for control points for areas (e.g., voting precincts), assuming one is studying a social phenomenon.

For reconciling census block data with voting district data, the computer program would take the voting precinct map and its control points and overlay them on top of the census block map and its control points. Then, one at a time for each voting precinct control point, it would calculate a reconciled estimate or interpolation. This estimate is equal to the weighted average of values of nearby control points on the census block map. PCDM allows the user to determine how many such points are used (e.g., the PCDM default is five). The more nearest points used, the more smoothing of the estimate surface.

The general formula for the weighted average (Hinze, 1989, p. 287) is as follows:

$$E_i = \frac{\sum\limits_{i=1}^{n} (w_i e_i)}{\sum\limits_{i=1}^{n} w_i}$$

In this equation E_i is the estimate of the given control point on the target surface (voting precincts) and w_i is the weight of e_i, which is the value of one of the n nearest control points on the source surface (census blocks). As a weighting method, the inverse of the distance from the target point to the ith source point (inverse squares weighting) or the inverse of the square of the distance (actual distance weighting) can be used. In a test of PCDM, Hinze (1989, pp. 204-295) found that using inverse squares weighting on the three nearest points was most effective in estimation.

Common Data Sources

PRODUCT FILES

Many of the boundary, line, attribute, datapoint, and other files needed by a GIS are available commercially as "canned" products. For instance, Atlas*Pro comes bundled with geographic files for countries of the world, cities of the world, Canadian provinces, U.S. states, major U.S. cities, interstate highways, U.S. telephone area code boundaries, U.S. standard metropolitan statistical area boundaries, Arbitron "areas of dominant influence" (ADIs), Nielsen "designated marketing areas" (DMAs), and five-digit ZIP code centroids. The makers of MapInfo also vend boundary files (counties, ZIP code areas, postal code areas, census consolidated subdivisions, census subdivisions, census tracts, census tract block groups, federal electoral districts, areas of dominant influence, designated market areas, metropolitan statistical areas, minor civil divisions, and census civil divisions), line files (highways by state or region, streets by county, railways by state or U.S.), point files (cities and towns, ZIP code centers, telephone area code centers), and attribute files (population, income, retail, and business data). International equivalents of these product files are under development by MapInfo at the time of this writing.

Data available in Lotus 1-2-3 .WK1 format or dBASE .DBF format can usually be brought into GIS attribute files and datapoint files, but geocoding may have to be done manually for data products not intended for GIS use. That is, the user has to add and fill in a new ID field linking each record to a feature or point in a corresponding geographic file.

ZIP code data are among the most common map-related data products, with a variety of vendors competing. Datatron Systems Inc. sells a dBASE .DBF format file of state, county, ZIP, and place names, packaged with royalty-free dBASE code for use of the data. ZIP/Clip is a large dBASE .DBF file of ZIP code information, with corresponding city, county, and state names and other data, packaged with Clipper routines (Clipper is a leading dBASE-compatible database manager). Melissa Data Corporation publishes a catalog of ZIP code and related data files. Customized Computer Typesetting Services provides city-county-state ZIP code information in .DBF and other formats.[3] Note that ZIP code files require frequent updating because of changes in postal zones; consequently, most vendors of ZIP code files also sell updates by subscription.

CENSUS PRODUCTS

There are a large number of census products available on computer tape, CD-ROM, online, and in hardcopy. For the 1990 census, the national map set includes some 65,000 county-level map sheets (about 20 per county). Access is coordinated by the U.S. Bureau of the Census, Data User Services Division. Subscriptions to the *Monthly Product Announcement* are free from Customer Services. The *Census Catalog and Guide: 1990* (S/N 003-024-07169-0) contains detailed information about Census Bureau products and services. The cost is $14 from the U.S. Superintendent of Documents.

Major product lines include the Census of Population and Housing, Current Population Reports, Current Housing Reports, Economic Censuses of Outlying Areas, Census of Agriculture, Annual Survey of Manufactures (ASM), Census of Manufactures, Census of Construction Industries, Current Construction Reports, Current Foreign Trade Reports, Census of Mineral Industries, Census of Retail Trade, Enterprise Statistics, Current Business Patterns Reports, and Current Government Reports. There are also many special data files, such as Public Law 94-171 data files, which contain counts used for decennial redistricting by the state governments, with information on population, race, Hispanic origin, and housing units. Normally, data are released first on computer tape, and later some but not all information is released on CD-ROM and other media. The online service, CENDATA (available on DIALOG, the largest online information vendor) contains many data tables such as are found in the print version of *Statistical Abstract of the United States*.

The Census Bureau also sells five plotter-generated map types: county block maps, P.L. 94-171 county block maps, voting district outline maps, census tract/block numbering area (BNA) maps, and county subdivision outline maps. Benefiting from the TIGER system, the Census Bureau is printing about 10 times as many maps for the 1990 census as it did for the 1980.

Numerous private vendors analyze, repackage, and resell census data. A leader in this group is the National Planning Data Corporation (NPDC).[4] Among the NPDC's census-related products are census estimates. The 1990 NPDC census estimates were only .58% different from the actual 1990 census nationwide, yet were available long before 1990 census data became available. The NPDC also provides custom extracts of census tapes, census reference books, consumer purchasing data, seminars, and other services, including its MAX^{3D} online data service and MapAnalyst mapping software.

TIGER FILES

The Bureau of the Census initiated the Topologically Integrated Geographic Encoding and Referencing system in 1983 for the 1990 census of population (Marx, 1990). TIGER is designed for GIS applications, supporting a variety of map types. Costing $350 million, containing 19 gigabytes of information on 37 CD-ROM disks, and supported by more than 70 commercial software vendors, TIGER is the first digitized street map of the entire United States. With it and accompanying software (e.g., Safari, from Geographic Data Technology Inc.) one can, for instance, highlight census boundaries, highlight street segments or water features, or view the extent of address ranges, using a mouse to point and click on the map, then view corresponding information in the data window. The TIGER data files and corresponding software illustrate geographic information systems: Spatial data on boundaries, roads, hydrology, railroads, and other features are available in conjunction with relational database files on names, descriptions, and other text and numeric data associated with map points, lines, and areas (Bishton, 1988).

TIGER/Line (T/L) map data are available on 125 high-density tapes or 38 CD-ROMs, covering the entire United States. These files are a digitized map database covering geographic areas and codes for all census designated places. The average size for TIGER/Line file data for one state is 400 megabytes, and about 6 MB for a typical county, though this varies widely. Also available are TIGER/DataBase (T/D) files, containing point, line, and area information extracted from the TIGER database, used to facilitate the input of TIGER data into geographic information systems. TIGER/GIS files contain the geographic information codes that allow one to assign names to areas without manual coding of labels. Finally, TIGER/Boundary files contain coordinate data for specific boundary sets such as 1990 state and county boundaries or census block numbering areas. Where digitized map data can be three-quarters of the expense of initiating a GIS, the availability of TIGER data provides substantial savings as well as power.

However, the U.S. Census Bureau does not sell software that utilizes TIGER data. Users must buy off-the-shelf mapping packages with TIGER support features, or must program their own. Atlas*GIS, for instance, supports street-based mapping using TIGER files using a TIGER conversion utility program sold at extra cost. Commercial vendors sometimes sell versions of TIGER files that have been enhanced for greater compatibility with their programs, as is the case for Atlas*Pro from Strategic Mapping, Inc. Dynamap/2000, sold through Strategic Mapping, Inc. (makers of the Atlas series of software), are enhanced TIGER files from GDT that have twice the number of streets with address ranges than the original census TIGER files.

Similarly, FMS/AC has a module called FMS/TIGER Plus that allows users to draw data from TIGER files, add new linear features to TIGER street maps, extract attribute data from newly created graphic features, implement address matching, retrieve data within a user-specified radius, and transfer information to other FMS/AC modules such as Street Maintenance and many others. Maps compatible with FMS/TIGER, FMS/AC, and AutoCAD are also sold by American Digital Cartography, Inc.[5]

TIGER supplants the computerized GBF/DIME files used in the 1980 census. The GBF/DIME files covered some 2% of the U.S. land area, but 60% of the population in 345 metropolitan and other developed areas. Due to primitive scanning techniques then used, DIME files are cartographically inaccurate but usually contain high-quality data for purposes of address matching, address geocoding, and even thematic mapping. DIME files are quite inexpensive. For a description of the data formats of DIME files, see Mather (1991, pp. 44-46). Updated versions of the GBF/DIME files were incorporated in TIGER. DIME files are sometimes used in conjunction with ETAK files, which are a commercial database of road centerline information compatible with GIS packages such as Arc/Info.

TIGER is not universally applicable, in spite of its many advantages. Circumstances in which it is *not* appropriate include RFD rural address system address geocoding, road construction or applications where high-precision coordinate accuracy is required, and spatial analysis for soil studies or land use. TIGER is not 100% accurate and, of course, roads, boundaries, and other data used by TIGER are constantly evolving. TIGER is based on street address ranges and is prohibited under Title 13 of the U.S. Code from containing individual addresses, and even the street ranges may require updating in given areas.

Another consideration in utilizing TIGER data is that it was first and foremost intended as a means to facilitate the census count. Therefore, certain conventions were included in the mapping that made for more ease in field counting but may not accurately represent field conditions. One convention to be aware of is the extension of dead-end streets to create closure within a wide area that would otherwise represent a single census block. This creates artificial "blocks" for census count purposes, but in reality these blocks do not exist because the road extensions are not there.

Many users will want to transfer TIGER data to a more conventional database format. This requires third-party utility software, such as Census Windows: TIGER Tools (GeoVision, Inc.). This utility, which runs under Windows or OS/2, can transfer TIGER file data to databases in such formats as dBASE, Excel, AutoCAD, MARS, GeoVision, and ASCII. It can extract 135 TIGER feature classes, match feature class codes, edit TIGER records, draw and control feature maps, output reformatted data, and/or link to Excel spreadsheets using DDE (Dynamic Data Exchange, a feature of Windows and OS/2). PC CAD Interface, from the same firm, is a similar but more specialized utility geared to transferring TIGER files to AutoCAD .DXF format for users of that leading computer-assisted design package.

CD-ROM ACCESS

TIGER/Line files, as mentioned, are available on CD-ROM from the Census Bureau (for the Macintosh or MS-DOS microcomputers with the Microsoft CD-ROM Extensions 2.0 or higher). There are many geographic-related CD-ROM products apart from the many produced by the Census Bureau. Illustrative products are mentioned here.

GEOdisc U.S. Atlas contains a digital representation of the United States on a scale of 1:2M. The maps include political boundaries, highways and railroads, waterways, and more, with a file of place and landmark names (more than a million entries) with coordinate information. It operates with Windows/On the World software, included on the disk, which allows data retrieval, display with zoom, and editing within the Microsoft Windows environment. The software can generate vector-mapped overlays, with output to color hardcopy devices or other Windows applications, including cut-and-paste of maps to other documents.

World Atlas contains more than 240 full-color maps with hundreds of pages of associated text information. As such, it is an electronic world fact book, including data from many U.S. and international agencies, covering geography, demography, government, economy, and communications. U.S. Atlas is a similar product for the United States.

ZipView accepts ASCII files containing ZIP code information and produces choropleth maps in up to six colors. ASCII files can be produced from Lotus 1-2-3, dBASE, or a word processor. Built-in software allows the user to zoom in to display regional, state, or local data, and to scroll across the map at the same magnification level. Users can also interrogate specific areas to pinpoint the ZIP code for that location. The purpose of ZipView is to track advertising leads geographically, but it can be used for any social science analysis that collects ZIP codes as one of the data fields.

ONLINE DATA SERVICES

A large variety of map-related online data services are available to social scientists. Many are found on DIALOG, the service of the nation's largest online information vendor. DIALOG can be accessed through a simple menu system shown in Figure 2.1. This menu leads to other choices, such as the Census Bureau's online database, CENDATA, itself governed by a menu shown in Figure 2.2. From the menu in Figure 2.1, the user would choose 5 (Database Selection), which leads further into the menu system and ultimately to a particular choice, such as CENDATA. On selection of CENDATA, CENDATA's opening menu, shown in Figure 2.2, is presented.

CENDATA is, of course, not the only online source of geographic data. GEOREF is also available on DIALOG as File 89. This database from the American Geological Institute covers worldwide literature on geology. Using the clause "IL=MAP?" within a DIALOG SELECT command for this file will retrieve maps. The clause "SF=USGS" will point the online search

32

```
Enter an option number and press ENTER to view information on any
item listed below; enter /NOMENU to move into Command Mode; or enter
a BEGIN command to search in a different database.

            1  Announcements (new databases, price changes, etc.)
            2  DIALOG HOMEBASE Features
            3  DIALOG Free File of the Month
            4  DIALOG Database Information and Rates
            5  Database Selection (DIALINDEX/OneSearch Categories)
            6  DIALOG Command Descriptions
            7  DIALOG Training Schedules and Seminar Descriptions
            8  DIALOG Services

Enter an option number, /NOMENU, or a BEGIN command and press ENTER.

    /H = Help        /L = Logoff        /NOMENU = Command Mode
```

Figure 2.1. Initial DIALOG Menu

to U.S. Geological Survey maps, reports, and other publications. Searching
by geographic coordinates is also possible.

LOCALIZED DATA SOURCES

The proliferation of affordable GIS packages for use on PCs has had the
peripheral effect of increasing the number and quality of databases available

```
     1  Introduction to Census Bureau Products and Services
     2  What's New in CENDATA (Including Economic Survey Release Dates)
     3  U.S. Statistics at a Glance (Including Economic Time Series Data)

     4  Press Releases
--------------------------------
     5  Census User News              ! If you're a new or infrequent !
     6  Product Information           ! user of the CENDATA menu       !
     7  CENDATA User Feedback         ! system, key HELP <cr> to learn!
     8  Profiles and Rankings         ! of the available short cuts in!
     9  Agriculture Data              ! using the system.             !
    10  Business Data                 = = = = = = = = = = = = = = = = =
    11  Construction and Housing Data ! For a listing and a location!
    12  Foreign Trade Data            ! key of all Census Bureau     !
    13  Governments Data              ! reports contained in CENDATA!
    14  International Data            ! in whole or in part, key     !
    15  Manufacturing Data           ! M1.2 <cr>                    !
    16  Population Data
--------------------------------
    17  Genealogical and Age Information
    18  1990 Census Information
    Enter choice:
```

Figure 2.2. CENDATA Main Menu

at the local level. Often these data are available at little or no cost to users and can be acquired in common formats.

Many states have designated geographic resource agencies. County-level GIS departments are a common and growing resource for parcel, boundary, and land-use databases. Often these agencies have census data already converted into commonly used GIS formats.

Other sources of street and address data are transportation-oriented agencies. Public transportation authorities will usually have a map base of collector streets and thoroughfares in a digital format. Local school boards and emergency response centers will likely have a very detailed street map database. Finally, the best source for mailing lists and parcel databases including data on land value, land use, and zoning will be the local property tax office.

3. MAP GRAPHICS

While manual mapping methods are still used and can prove quite satisfactory for certain social science purposes (see Southall & Oliver, 1990), computerized mapping is now the norm. For many social scientists, computer mapping is a matter of selecting a software package that contains built-in boundary files related to one's course or research, has relevant built-in databases, and can display or print basic choropleth maps, perhaps with custom labeling and symbols (e.g., arrows) added by the user. Thus for teachers and researchers in international affairs and foreign policy, Mandell (1991) has reviewed some 20 software packages that fulfill these needs. For instance, PC Globe comes with built-in world, continent, and country maps as well as a large quantitative database. The *Time* Magazine Compact Almanac comes with continent maps and a large textual database.

This popular map-related software is of three types. Electronic atlas software such as PC Globe allows students (and researchers) to see data patterns graphically as displayed on world, continent, country, or state maps. With electronic atlases data may be displayed easily and in some cases the instructor/researcher can add new data. The second type is general educational software, in which maps are keyed to tutorials and/or textual databases as a form of interactive lesson or reference work, as in Compton's Multimedia Encyclopedia. The third type is desktop publishing software with a mapping component, such as MapArt. These are files of outline maps that the user can customize with labels and symbols of his or her choosing, and sometimes by filling in hatch or color patterns in a choropleth map related to a spreadsheet or other database.

Most GIS software, in contrast, stores map information in vector form based on a given coordinate system. This allows the user to move from one projection to another, to set scaling, to use multiple overlays, and to compute spatial statistics (e.g., interpoint distances) easily. The database component of GIS allows users to frame spatially related queries, such as creating the subset of all records within a 10-mile radius of a given coordinate. These and other advanced features differentiate GIS software from popular mapping software, though many packages exist on the fuzzy border between the two.

Digitizing Maps

Normally, maps are purchased in digitized boundary file form. GIS software such as Atlas*GIS provides an optional module (ATLAS*IM-PORT/EXPORT) for translating among a variety of boundary file formats if the initial format of a purchased boundary file is not what is needed. Alternatively, GIS software makes it is quite possible for social scientists to create their own maps using digitizing techniques. Indeed, this is often necessary when studying other than the standard political units: tribal areas in anthropology, service areas in policy analysis, or areas of influence in sociology. For an overview of acquiring and entering digital data into a GIS, see Dangermond (1989).

Professional surveyors now use computerized systems in the field to develop maps with high precision. For instance, the Trimble GPS system, which is the industry leader, includes a built-in survey database manager that can store and graphically display all control points in the area of interest. The database module allows users to click on any two points with a mouse and get the distance between them. Disks with NGS and USGS control points may be used. Fieldwork is supported by "walk-about" kinematic surveying, using receivers that collect data for profiling, ground modeling, and contouring. Accompanying menu-driven software (TRIMVEC-Plus) automates the handling of field data, including baseline processing, loop closure, network adjustment, and report generation. The software also supports conversion to state plane and local coordinates.

Social scientists, however, rarely develop maps from field observations. Rather, if they do not purchase boundary files outright, they work from maps provided by government units and private vendors. The quality in precision of such source maps should be considered. Often they were originally developed for thematic use with little or no ground control. Edge matching of different map sheets can become a problem. Digitizing is the manual transfer of these hardcopy maps to an electronic form usable by the GIS to be employed. Digitizing is a very labor-intensive activity, and the quality of the final product will depend on the accuracy of the source maps and the attention of the digitizing technician. Many packages offer functions that assist in correcting problems with edge matching. Any digitizing project utilizing several map sheets will probably require some manual correction of map or data entry error.

Roots is an example of a digitizing program used in academic settings. Operating on MS-DOS, Macintosh, or Sun platforms, Roots supports a variety of digitizing tablets and monitors. The general procedure is to use a mouse or digitizing tablet to click on points or on chains (series of points forming a line or connecting back to the origin to form a polygon). The user then assigns identifiers to each point, line, or polygon. Lines and points may be edited to remove inadvertent false entries or to move entries. A control point system allows the user to then relate the map to an external coordinate system. At the end, of course, the map is saved onto disk, from which it may be converted into a variety of map formats.

CONTROL POINTS

Control points are spots defined by a given longitude and latitude in relation to the coordinate system in use by the given GIS. In isopleth mapping, control points determine the shape of contour lines. That is, the computer connects all control points exhibiting in the same value range for the variable being studied. In distribution maps, control points are the centers for the circles or other symbols used to indicate various levels of the given variable. When isopleth or distribution maps are to be used, it is necessary to map control points to create a point file. Points may be census block centroids, city centers, or locations of measurement stations in the field, depending on the type of study.

SCANNING

An option for digital map building of growing relevance is map scanning. Map scanning is similar in process to document scanning, but is not the simple solution to labor-intensive manual digitizing that might be expected. The high cost of quality map scanning equipment leaves it primarily in the domain of contract service bureaus; however, the technology does offer a high level of precision, even for large-format originals. Color scanning is a possibility and, most important, the process can be tailored to the needs of GIS-type applications. The scanning process creates a raster image ranging is resolution from 200 to 500 dots per inch. In order to accomplish GIS tasks, the raster image must be converted to a vector format to allow graphic information to be used and manipulated in a GIS environment. The conversion process may involve manual selection and manipulation of image features performed at a workstation or may be performed by the software as a batch process. As imaging technology advances, scanning will likely become a more common mode of geobased data entry in the future.

Graphics File Formats, Conversion

While almost all GIS packages use vector-based maps, there is no single standard for storing vector information in computer files. Perhaps the most widespread standard is the .DXF (Drawing Interchange Format) format used for import-export by the AutoCAD computer-assisted design package (which also uses its own native .DWG drawing format files) and the related FMS/AC GIS software. However, there are many other formats. MapInfo also imports and exports geographic files in .DXF format as well as using its own .MBI data format. Intergraph uses the .DGN format as well as the .SIF Standard Interchange Format, which is also used by many other packages. GisPlus uses the .PCX raster graphics format made popular by PC Paintbrush. Harvard Geographics and Harvard Graphics use the .SYM and .CHT formats, although they interface with others (.EPS Encapsulated PostScript, .HPGL Hewlett Packard Graphics Language, .CGM Computer Graphics Metafile, .PCX). Atlas Graphics uses the .BNA format.

Users should note that some formats are for raster images and some for vector data. Vector formats, which dominate GIS, include .CGM (Computer Graphics Metafile) used by Aldus's PageMaker and Xerox's Ventura Publisher desktop publishing packages. Other vector formats are .PCI, the Lotus 1-2-3 graphing format; .PGL, the Hewlett Packard Graphics Language, HPGL); .WMF, the Microsoft Windows Metafile, which has a 64K limit; and .DRW, the Micrografx DRAW file, another Windows format not limited to 64K and supported by Ventura Publisher, Legend, and other publishing programs. Raster images are associated with .TIF (Tagged Image File Format, TIFF), originated by PageMaker and used by many scanning devices; and with .PCX, the PC Paintbrush graphics format. There is also an .EPS Encapsulated PostScript format that incorporates both vector and raster data, displaying raster images on the screen but using vector data to drive printer output.

The U.S. Geological Survey (USGS) uses the .DLG (Digital Line Graph) file format. These files are far cheaper than producing a new precise land base and are available for the entire United States. Version 3.0 of the DLF files carry considerable attribute as well as topological information. The USGS National Space Technology Laboratory has converted .DLG files to the .DXF format used by AutoCAD and FMS/AC, showing how these files can be employed as a low-cost municipal land base. Companies such as American Digital Cartography sell DLG quadrangle maps in .DWG, .DGN, and .DXF formats.[6]

Tralaine is a PC map coordinate conversion utility that can be used to convert coordinates during a file copy process among any of nine formats. These include .DXF (AutoCAD, FMS/AC), .DLG-3 (USGS), .GEN (Arc/Info), .SDF (standard data format, as from dBASE), DLMTXT (ASCII comma-delimited format, as from dBASE), .BNA (Atlas*Graphics and Atlas*GIS), .MBI (MapInfo), and others. Options allow direct conversion of AutoCAD .DWG files without need to create intervening .DXF files. HiJaak is another utility package that can convert among common graphics formats.

4. ANALYTIC MAPPING

Types of Maps

REFERENCE MAPS

The basic map type is the reference map, which shows the boundaries of certain features (areas) and locates various objects within each, usually labeling each object. Highway maps are of this type, for instance, locating such objects as roads, highway exits, municipalities, and recreation areas. Topographic maps are a particular type of reference map in which the objects are land surface features such as roads, streams and water drainage lines, and railways. Although reference maps are conceptually simple, issues do arise. For instance, computerized labeling may be accomplished at any of three levels of increasing sophistication: location of the label at the polygon centroid; testing to make sure the centroid is within the polygon, and locating the label in an alternate spot if it is not; and testing for inclusion and also autoadjusting the label horizontally so as much of the label as possible is printed within the polygon (Roessal, 1989).

The conceptual simplicity of reference maps means they can be purchased as clip art and manipulated as one would any other graphic image, adding labels, colors, and symbols, but not performing GIS operations. Figure 4.1 is a reference map of the United Kingdom produced using MapArt, a leading map clip art package.

CHOROPLETH MAPS

Perhaps the most familiar type of mapping is choropleth mapping, in which features (areas) on the map are colored or shaded according to some key so that the nature of shading reflects the intensity of some variable being mapped. These are sometimes also called thematic maps or simply shaded maps, although the term *thematic map* may include distribution maps also. Derived from the Greek words for place (*choros*) and value (*pleth*), choropleth mapping is illustrated in Figure 4.2, which shows the Wallace vote for president versus both the Republican (Nixon) and Democratic (Humphrey) candidates. This figure is produced by the Elections program and shows the vote for Wallace (an independent, anti-civil rights candidate) in 1968 Alabama. In a political map, for instance, the darkness of shading of map areas might signify the degree of support for a given presidential candidate. For further reading on thematic maps, see Cuff and Mattson (1982).

Depending on the mapping software, shading may reflect not only the magnitude of numeric attributes but also different values of a character attribute such as religious affiliation (Catholic, Protestant, Jew, for instance). For instance, the GeoCoast system of the National Oceanic and Atmospheric Administration uses Census Bureau TIGER digitized map files and other data to generate thematic atlases showing trends in national coastal resources (seven such map volumes had been published as of 1990). Choropleth maps normally use equal-area projection.

Area bias can occur in choropleth maps because, by nature, they depict an entire geographic area in a single hatching or color pattern. That is, choropleth maps make no accommodation for differences in standard deviation (heterogeneity versus homogeneity) of data within an area. In a choropleth map of population density, for instance, a desert area where everyone lives in a central city might be depicted the same as an agricultural area where the same size population is spread evenly throughout the region.

Although the subject has been much studied, there is no consensual method for determining how to partition a continuous variable into a set of classes (Paslawski, 1984). A common but arbitrary method is to divide the data range into equal portions according to the number of class intervals desired. The constant interval method can result in wildly disproportionate shares of cases in the different ranges. Using the standard deviation can avoid this, assuming normally distributed data, but results are equally arbitrary. An approach that seeks seemingly natural divisions is to group data such that within-class variance is minimized. This is done by Jenks (1977) using an algorithm developed by Fisher (1958), and Smith (1986) uses a goodness-of-variance-fit (GVF) test (see Dent, 1990, pp. 163-165).[7] Others advocate selection of the classification scheme that maximizes the F value in one-way analysis of variance (i.e., the ratio of between groups variance to variance within groups; see Dent, 1990, pp. 161-162). However, these more complex methods are frequently ignored in general use.

In general, choropleth maps usually display three to eight value categories of a variable. Eight is thought to be an upper limit in terms of the average map reader's threshold of discrimination (Jenks, 1963, p. 20). That is, if continuous data cannot be reduced to a number of categories in this range without undue loss of data, choropleth mapping is inappropriate. As the number of categories increases, it becomes more and more difficult for the map user to discern the meaning of different hatching and color patterns or even to differentiate them one from another. Figure 4.3 illustrates one approach to this problem: printing actual values in areas and using a scale-type legend, in this case one measuring average dollars per household. The legend graphically shows that the white areas represent a broader income range than do the darker areas.

Many studies have shown that users readily equate darker areas with larger amounts, a fact that can confuse users when mapping qualitative variables (e.g., primary religious affiliation) that are not ordered by amount (Antes & Chang, 1990). Note also that backgrounds should be light, because some users equate light with "more" if a dark background is used (McGranaghan, 1989).

Choropleth maps may be classed or unclassed. Classed choropleth maps have a finite number of discrete hatching patterns or gray tones or colors and any given record is assigned to one of these classes. As in any system of classification, information is lost as data are tipped into one category or another regardless of whether they are at the low or high end of their given category. Unclassed choropleth maps, in contrast, use a unique hatching pattern, gray scale, or color tone to indicate the unique level of each area with respect to the variable being measured. That is, if per capita income is measured, one of three things will be done:

1. The separation of lines on the hatch pattern will be adjusted proportionally to per capita income, with the least income corresponding to the most spacing.

2. In the dot-density technique, a number of dots will be placed randomly throughout the area exactly proportional to the amount of per capita income.
3. In a color system, an exact tone will be painted whose spectral position corresponds to the amount of per capita income.

Unclassed choropleth maps are computation-intensive and have come about through computerized mapping. There is some evidence unclassed choropleth maps can be understood more accurately than classed maps with five or fewer classes (Peterson, 1979). There is also some evidence that cross-line hatching is more easily interpreted than solid color pattern or gray tone sequences (Mak & Coulson, 1991), provided the hatching pattern is progressively denser as amount increases.

UBC Maps. UBC maps are unclassed bivariate choropleth maps. These attempt to display the spatial distribution of two variables using crosshatch patterns. Figure 4.4 shows an unclassed univariate map. In comparison, in UBC maps the spacing of vertical lines is indicative of the amount of one variable, with closer spacing proportional to greater amount. Likewise, the spacing of the horizontal lines forming the hatch pattern is made proportional to a second variable. UBC maps are complex, but studies have found they perform adequately in allowing users to estimate values, contrary to early impressions in the cartographic community that UBC maps imposed too great a burden on the map reader (Lavin & Archer, 1984).[8] There is some evidence that slightly higher accuracy of estimation is obtained if the UBC map is accompanied by a matrix legend with discrete ranges (Aspaas & Lavin, 1989). That is, it may be better to have discrete classes of separation rather than a continuous range, and the legend should show the crosshatch patterns produced by the intersection of the horizontal and vertical classes.

Dasymetric Maps. Dasymetric maps are a type of choropleth map in which natural boundaries are used instead of political or other official boundaries. In an urban setting, for instance, natural boundaries might be formed by parks, areas of multiunit dwellings, industrial zones, and so on. Displaying a variable such as population density in choropleth maps based on political boundaries averages the population densities for these disparate natural areas. Dasymetric mapping is an attempt to delineate these natural areas and use them as a basis for choropleth mapping, so, for instance, parks with no residential population are not averaged in with areas of multifamily dwellings to create a misleading areal mean characteristic of single-family residential areas. Dasymetric mapping may require the researcher to custom

Figure 4.1. Reference Map of the United Kingdom, Produced Using MapArt
SOURCE: Used by permission of MicroMaps Software.

digitize natural areas, but this is recommended when the variables under study have discrete rather than continuous boundaries that do not correspond to political and administrative boundaries.

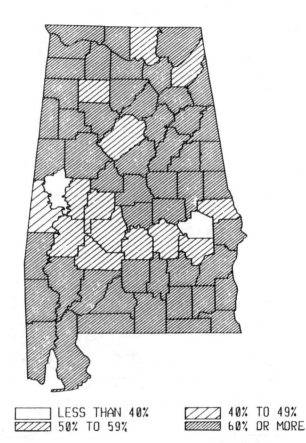

 CTYPCT ☐ LESS THAN 40% ▨ 40% TO 49%
▨ 50% TO 59% ▨ 60% OR MORE

Figure 4.2. Choropleth Map of 1968 Wallace Vote, Produced Using Elections
SOURCE: Reproduced courtesy of David L. Martin.

Block Maps. Block maps are a three-dimensional variation of choropleth maps. Also called *prism maps* and *oblique stepped-surface maps*, block maps use an oblique viewing angle and three-dimensional representation such that the height of an area corresponds to the amount of the variable being studied. There is the obvious problem with prism maps that areas with smaller values may not be visible if located behind areas with larger values. This defect can be avoided by using *elevated point maps*, in which "pins" of varying height are depicted arising from the center of each area. Elevated point maps, however, are more difficult to apprehend because the viewer's eye must move from the top of the pin to the base from which it arises to see the connection between amount and area. In block maps, in contrast, the entire shape of the base area is shown in elevated form with height proportional to amount. The viewer's eye is drawn to the top of given areas, viewing amount and recognizing the area by its shape simultaneously. In the stereoscopic map variant of block maps, two block maps are drawn parallel for stereoscopic viewing for true three-dimensional effect (Monmonier, 1982, pp. 126-128).

Area Cartograms. Area cartograms are a third variant of choropleth maps in which the two-dimensional boundaries of geographic units are distorted so that the surface area of each unit is proportional to the amount of the value being measured. A map of the world in which the size of countries is proportionate to GNP is an example of this. If values are too disparate, some units with low values may be too small to recognize and proportions within the map may become so distorted that it is no longer understandable in geographic terms the user will recognize, particularly if preservation of the external boundary is not a constraint in cartogram construction. An alternative is the noncontiguous area cartogram, which maintains the shape of regions (e.g., counties), sizes them according to magnitude on some variable (e.g., population percentage), and then locates these shapes noncontiguously such that their outside edges conform to the outline of the area (e.g., state) being analyzed (Monmonier, 1982, pp. 123-124). For a discussion of cartogram creation, see Raisz (1935) and Tobler (1968).

DISTRIBUTION MAPS

Distribution maps use various symbols to show how one or more attributes vary within each feature (area) on a map. *Pin mapping*, or incidence mapping, is a term for the simplest distribution mapping, in which points are overlaid on a base map to show, for instance, the location of murders in a given municipality. However, both points and lines can be varied in width, color, style, and other display characteristics to indicate the relative presence or absence of one or more attributes, much as different colors and hatch patterns are used in thematic maps to display attribute data. For this reason some packages refer to "thematic maps for point data" when referring to distribution maps. A common distribution map example is to show the distribution of population by displaying circles of increasing size to signify municipalities of increasing population. For instance, William Bowen and Eugene Turner (Department of Geography, California State University—

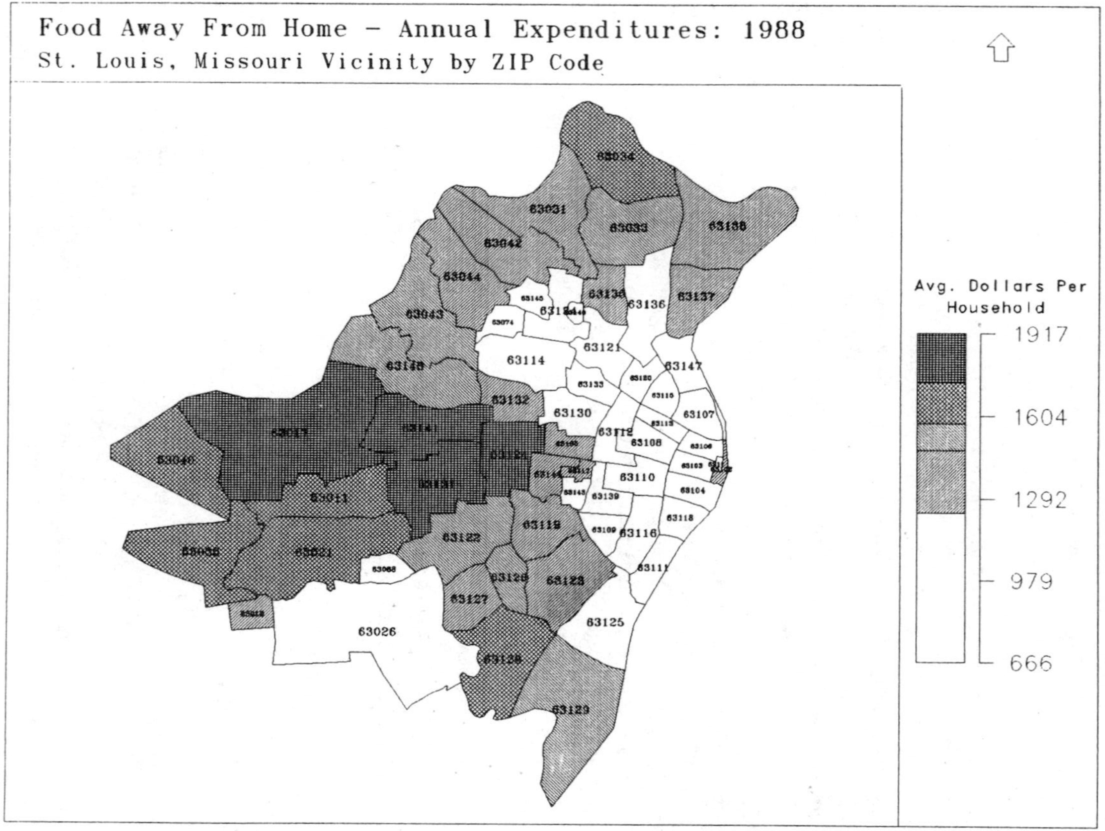

Figure 4.3. Choropleth Map With Superimposed Values and Scale Legend, Produced Using MapAnalyst

SOURCE: Used by permission of the National Planning Data Corporation.

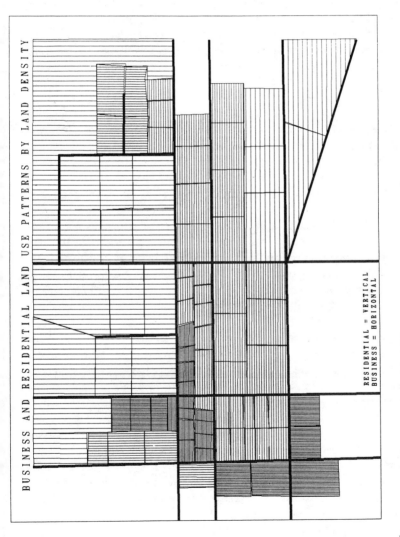

BUSINESS AND RESIDENTIAL LAND USE PATTERNS BY LAND DENSITY

RESIDENTIAL = VERTICAL
BUSINESS = HORIZONTAL

Figure 4.4. Unclassed Choropleth Map

45

Northridge) have used ATLAS*MapMaker to create point distribution maps on slavery. Points are county centroids and slave counts are represented as a series of progressively darker dot or circle symbols keyed to number of slaves.

Many other examples can be cited. The location of properties with bank mortgages could be mapped to gather information on possible bank redlining policies. One could compare the distribution of points, say, service delivery offices, with such overlays as transportation routes or to an overlay of the distribution of service requests. The National Institute on Drug Abuse uses GIS to match the distribution of AIDS-related client contacts with supplies of condoms, bleach, and other disease-fighting agents. Police can map the daytime and nighttime distribution of burglaries to create different patrol patterns for different time periods.

Use of Symbols. In addition to varying the width and other attributes of points and lines to denote variable amounts, the font and size of labels can be used for this purpose. Road maps usually use larger fonts proportional to city size when labeling cities, for instance. Also, to take a political science example, different fonts can be used to distinguish one type of control point (e.g., mayor-council cities) from another type of control point (e.g., city manager-council cities). Use of solid circles of varying sizes is a common method of implementing a distribution map. Dot-distribution maps that employ uniform-size small dots to convey a certain amount (e.g., 100,000 registered voters) do convey variations in spatial density effectively, but users usually find it impossible to estimate the original data values. As a rule, map users underestimate the number of dots on dot-distribution maps and underestimate the differences between areas with different dot densities (Provin, 1977).

In contrast, perceptual experimentation has validated proportional circle maps as a type having a high degree of pattern recognition and consistency among map readers (Jenks, 1975). Moreover, although users also underestimate circle sizes, absolute scaling may still be used, provided clear and appropriate legends are employed (Chang, 1980). One must select a sizing scheme such that the smallest control point values will correspond to a dot size that is still visible, while the largest value must correspond to a circle size that is not so large as to overlap and obscure other multiple control points. Also, even if there is plenty of room for display, use of larger dots may falsely imply that there are large amounts of the phenomenon being studied, when in fact the phenomenon is relatively rare (e.g., ax murder). Clear legends with each circle size shown next to its value equivalent are essential.

Dot-density maps such as the map of Washington population shown in Figure 4.5 use dots of the same size to indicate one or a given number of a phenomenon. A single dot indicates that amount of the phenomenon at that location. If location is not known, the dot is located randomly within the area. Each dot must represent a large enough number of the phenomenon that there will not be too much coalescence (overprinting of dots in denser areas). Likewise, if each dot represents too large a number, dot density will be sparse, misleadingly suggesting the phenomenon is rare. Such maps should use the smallest amount per dot that still does not involve significant coalescence. Selection of dot size and unit value may be aided by using the Mackay nomograph (Mackay, 1949; Robinson et al., 1984, p. 304).

When circles are made a lighter shade with a dark circumference, then points can overlap or be contained one within another and still convey the intended information. Bivariate distributions can be shown using pie circles. For instance, the size of circles could denote amount of real estate wealth in each area, and each circle could be shown with a pie-chart slice indicating minority-owned real estate. In more complex situations, the circle may be divided into many pie slices (e.g., each representing a different land use). Distribution maps can help visualize multiple variables simultaneously. A map of income patterns, for instance, could use M and F as symbols to map the gender of people in a sample survey. The size of these symbols might represent the salaries of each. Color could be used to indicate rate of change in salary.

Various GIS packages may support alternatives to circle symbols. Proportional spheres or cubes are sometimes used in place of circles. For that matter, actual numerals showing actual amounts may be used as symbols, perhaps scaled in fonts proportional to amount. Also, in the repeated symbols method, multiple symbols (e.g., boxes or pictorials such as oil barrels) are attached at points to which they refer, with the number of symbols proportionate to amount. This is equivalent to bar graphing, except the multisymbol "bars" are located geographically at appropriate map positions. Sometimes monthly data for a given year are represented by locating small 12-month vertical bar graphs at the locations of the cities or areas to which they refer.

Flow lines are often used to show migration, trade, and other intercourse between areas. As with circle maps, flow lines can be sized proportional to the amount of flow. Flow maps sometimes pattern flow lines along literal paths of movement, such as trade routes, but more often only origin and destination are shown, using an aesthetically curving but arbitrary path of connection.

ISARITHMIC MAPS

Isolines are lines that join control points of equal value. These values may be interval-level measurements (amount of income), ratios (per capita income), or even correlation coefficients (correlation of income to education). Isometric lines are lines connecting equal metric values, such as contour lines showing elevations above sea level. Isopleths or isopleth lines are isolines where the values being joined are ratios, such as population per square mile. Isarithmic maps are maps based on isometric or isopleth lines. However, often this class of maps is referred to as isopleth maps, regardless of isoline type.

Isopleth maps are a familiar type, though most often encountered in weather maps of frontal systems, or in geographic maps such as those of the National Geodetic Survey often used by hikers. Isopleth maps connect like points on a map with contour lines, and for this reason they are also known as contour maps. For instance, census blocks in the same median income range might be connected to show areas of wealth and poverty. The areas demarcated by isarithmic lines may be left blank or filled in with dot-density equivalents, gray scale tones, or colors. Physical maps, for instance, often use hypsometric tints—a color code ranging from green (low) to yellow to brown (high). In elevation maps, some misinterpret green to mean lush greenery, whereas it may indicate desert lowlands. Kummler and Groop (1990) have found that using a rainbow sequence of colors, with red representing high and violet representing low, is a more effective method of isopleth map representation than competing methods.

Isopleth maps are particularly useful in situations where choropleth maps would exaggerate the difference across a boundary. That is, marginal changes in the variable being measured (e.g., population density) may throw a given geographic unit into one category or another. Choropleth mapping hatches or colors each geographic area according to its category. The effect may be to suggest sharp changes in a variable such as population density as one crosses the boundary from one geographic unit to another. Isopleth maps, in contrast, show the actual contour lines of the geographic distribution of a value category. When these are superimposed on a layer showing the geographic boundaries, one can get a better understanding of the relationship between boundaries and values. Of course, to do this one must have data on many points within each geographic unit so that the contour lines can be drawn.

Figure 4.6, an isopleth map of world infant mortality, is presented to illustrate some of the problems of isopleth presentations. Infant mortality is

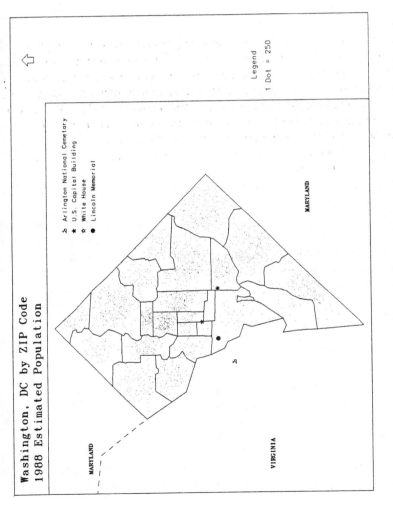

Washington, DC by ZIP Code
1988 Estimated Population

♨ Arlington National Cemetery
★ U.S. Capitol Building
☆ White House
● Lincoln Memorial

MARYLAND

MARYLAND

VIRGINIA

Legend

1 Dot = 250

Figure 4.5. Dot-Density Map of Population in Washington, D.C., Produced Using MapAnalyst

SOURCE: Used by permission of the National Planning Data Corporation.

a subject that can vary widely even in closely adjacent places, such as slums with high infant mortality adjacent to wealthy neighborhoods with low infant mortality. Likewise, cities or other sites with high infant mortality may be situated adjacent to deserts or bodies of water with virtually zero infant mortality. This is the case with Figure 4.6, where infant mortality contours are imposed on broad areas of the South Atlantic and Indian Ocean, where the actual infant mortality rate is close to zero. Proper use of isopleth maps presumes the existence of a high degree of spatial autocorrelation where one might plausibly expect geographic gradients, as in rainfall, pollution, or farm income.[9]

Fishnet Maps. These are the isarithmic equivalent of block maps, using an oblique three-dimensional view to depict continuous values, such that height correlates with amount being measured. There is some evidence, however, that fishnet maps are less easily interpretable than color-tone isopleth maps (Kummler & Groop, 1990). Surfer is an example of an inexpensive mapping program that produces three-dimensional fishnet maps as well as two-dimensional isopleth contour maps (see Dent, 1990: 232).

PROFILES

Profiles are isarithmic traces taken in a vertical direction. Profile traces are perpendicular planes that, in the case of data on the earth, show the surface and subsurface strata along a given line. To make an area map, one must situate two or more profiles perpendicular to each other to form an isometric block diagram. This allows the user to view the elevations of the surface and of each subsurface stratum. Data are not restricted to geology, however. The strata can show the areal distribution of various age cohorts, for instance. With computer assistance, traces may now be taken from any angle, rotation, or viewing elevation.

Buffers

The demarcation of a map area as a buffer is a useful application of the backward data capture ability of GIS. A buffer is an area of measured distance from a selected map element (point, line, polygon), such as a corridor on either side of a line representing a highway or a radius around the perimeter of a map region. Applications of buffering may include the generation of a mailing list of properties within a given distance of a site and the establishment of an area subject to height restrictions around an airport. Some GIS

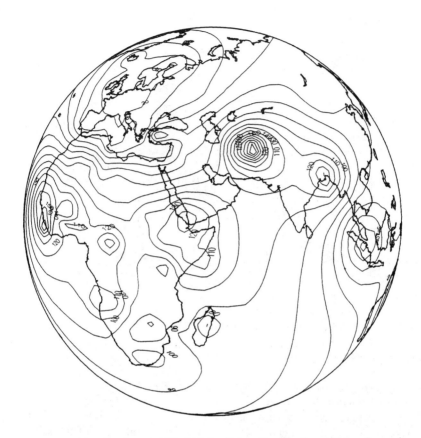

Figure 4.6. Isopleth Map of World Infant Mortality, Produced Using Sygraph
SOURCE: Used by permission of Systat, Inc.

packages, such as Arc/Info, can generate buffers around any of the three map elements; others are limited to buffers around points and lines only.

Overlays

Nearly all mapping packages support map overlays. For instance, a file of ZIP code areas can be superimposed on a file of county boundaries, then a city point overlay added, and then a highway line overlay added. To take

52

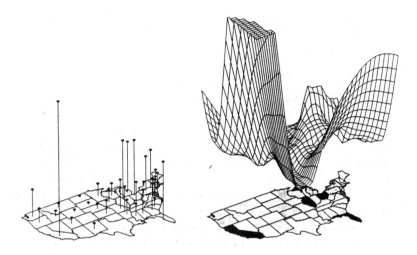

Figure 4.7. Raised Pin Map, Produced Using Sygraph; Fishnet Map on Choropleth Base

SOURCE: Used by permission of Systat, Inc.

a social science illustration, Dutt, Kendrick, and Nash (1979) overlaid a voting pattern map on a census map of Akron, Ohio, to analyze the Carter vote in the 1976 presidential elections. Of course, only files of the same projection can be overlaid. (In Atlas*GIS, projections are changed with the File-Geographic-Tools-Project command.) The completed overlay map is placed in a separate file, leaving the original files unchanged. In most systems, the overlay file will take up nearly as much disk space as the sum of separate files used for overlays.

In Atlas*GIS such overlays can be created easily. The user first chooses the largest file using the File-Geographic-UseAs command. The UseAs element in the command assures the original file will not be changed. The user then gives the File-Geographic-Tools-Append command to select the second file to be included. He or she is then given the option to "Reject Duplicates," which means incoming features with IDs in the first file will be dropped. Alternatively, the user may "Replace Duplicates." This step is repeated for as many layers as desired.

It should be noted that the accuracy of map information is related inversely to the number of map layers, the accuracy of the map layers, and the extent to which errors occur at the same position in several map layers. That is, cumulative errors occur with map overlaying. Newcomer and Szajgin (1984) have proposed a method of calculating the upper and lower accuracy bounds of composite overlay maps. This method, however, requires knowing the probability that a correct value occurs in a given layer at a given location. Because generally this is not known, this method is not widely used.

Modeling With Maps

One can perform limited mapping functions using conventional statistical software that has provided mapping in its graphics component. Systat/Sygraph, for instance, supports choropleth maps, isopleth maps, and three-dimensional block maps.[10] It is also possible to interface conventional statistics packages with GIS software. Southall and Oliver (1990, p. 151) present an SAS data step to output a command file usable by a GIS system (in this case, GIMMS; see Mather, 1991: chap. 4), including an example of mapping unemployment in the United Kingdom. However, statistical packages, including Systat/Sygraph, generally lack the versatility of GIS software in moving among coordinate systems, implementing overlays, digitizing capabilities, and other aspects of full GIS software. The use of GIS software in modeling is discussed in the sections that follow.

Although apparently not incorporated into existing GIS packages, a variety of slide-show packages exist that can animate a series of maps through time or another variable. When used with three-dimensional maps, map animation allows visual analysis of four dimensions simultaneously.

DATA SEARCHING

To a certain extent, GIS allows visual searching. Zoom and pan capabilities allow broad overviews of map features, lines, attributes, and points, followed up by detailed examination. Maps may be viewed from a variety of angles, sometimes in three dimensions. The ability of GIS to limit the scope of a data search to a defined subset of the geographic database is an efficient means of locating information. Termed *backward data capture*, the delineation of a geographic area within the database as a whole automatically filters out records with like values that may be superfluous to the matter under analysis. For instance, while racial migration on a citywide basis may not be readily detectable over a relatively short period of time, it may become more recognizable within chosen neighborhoods within a very short time frame. Combined with map animation, visual searching can be tantamount to simulated tours of geographic distributions of information.

Value searching is also easy with GIS. Thus in a map in which features are states and datapoints are ZIP code centroids, one could locate almost instantly all datapoints with median salary more than $25,000 and percentage black more than 20%. Name searching is the character variable equivalent. One could display all places containing the term *field*, for example. Likewise, in a GIS with data on individuals with residence locations as points, one could find the point representing "Roger S. Smith" instantly. Value searching has uses ranging from providing background for policy discussions to dispatching help for particular individuals. Most cities with populations above 100,000 now have computerized dispatching systems such that the location of 911 emergency calls can be identified in a second (Parent & Church, 1989, p. 16).

Address matching, a special form of value searching, is a feature of many GIS programs, such as Atlas*GIS. Address matching allows combination of data sets based on records that share a common address.

Proximity searching is one of the useful capabilities of GIS systems. It can be used in a regional ride-share program to match commuters and rides, matching both home and workplace proximities. A political campaign can use proximity searching to generate a list of all people who registered Democratic and who are located within a five-mile radius of a given campaign headquarters.

All these forms of searching are extended by geographic information systems based on local area (or other) networks, which allow multiple users at remote locations to access the system. As with all networked systems, various users can get different access and/or editing privileges using a system of passwords and other security provisions.

SUMMARY STATISTICS

A wide variety of summary statistics have been developed for topological applications. Unfortunately, most mapping packages are very weak in this area. Atlas*GIS, for example, implements centroid computation and can be manipulated to compute areal averages and geographic means, but at this writing supports none of the other forms of elementary statistical analysis discussed below, much less more specialized forms.

Distance. Given rectangular coordinates **x** and **y** for two points, the Pythagorean theorem solves for distance, *d*:

$$d = \sqrt{(x_2 - x_1)^2 + (y_1 - y_2)^2}$$

That is, the sum of the squares of two sides of a right triangle equal the square of the hypotenuse, which is the distance. Note that this method works in three dimensions if a third set of coordinates, **z**, is added as the term "+ $(z_1 - z_2)^2$" under the radical.

Shape Measures. A number of statistics have been devised to summarize the shape of a region. The form ratio is a measure of a unit's compactness in terms of elongation (measured in terms of area in relation to width):

$$FR \cong 1.27(A/L^2)$$

In this formula *A* is the area of the unit and *L* is the distance between the unit's two most distant points. The form ratio, the derivation of which is discussed in Selkirk (1982, pp. 53-54), varies from 0 to 1, with low values indicating a highly elongated shape and a high value indicating a very compact shape. For instance, Czechoslovakia has a form ratio of .28 and Romania has a form ratio of .56.

The compactness ratio is a measure of a unit's compactness in terms of the radius, *R*, of the smallest circle that will circumscribe its perimeter:

$$\text{Compactness} \cong 0.32A/R^2$$

The compactness ratio, which has been used in analysis of voting districts, assumes values very close to those of the form ratio.

The radius ratio is a measure of a unit's compactness in terms of the ratio of the radius, *r*, of the largest circle that can be contained within the unit's borders, to *R*, the radius of the smallest circle that can circumscribe the unit. Thus the radius ratio is simply *r/R*.

The circularity ratio, sometimes taken as a measure of a unit's compactness, is better thought of as a measure of the convolutedness of a unit's borders (based on the ratio of perimeter to area):

$$CR \cong 12.6A/p^2$$

In this formula A is the area of the unit and p is its perimeter or border length. The circularity ratio varies from 0 to 1, with 1 being a unit whose border is a circle. The more convoluted the border, the more the circularity ratio will approach zero. The circularity ratio, with its focus on perimeter length, may well rank units differently than the preceding ratios.

Areal Averages. The simplest and by far most common summary statistics used in mapping are areal averages. Density measures are areal averages in which the number of phenomena is divided by the number of area units in the polygon, such as population per square mile. Another example would be wheat production per acre. Naturally, when the acreage of an entire area is used as the denominator in such statistics, gross misrepresentation can occur. That is, it may well be that the actual acreage used for wheat production is only a small fraction of the acreage of the area as a whole.

One way to deal with this problem is the center of gravity approach. A symbol of varying size can be used to depict different amounts of the variable under study (e.g., crop productivity). Where crops are distributed evenly throughout an area, the symbol is located at the geometric center of the area. However, where this is not the case, the symbol is located at the center of gravity. The center of gravity can be defined as the centroid (see below) or by variants on this algorithm. However, some prefer to use the location of greatest density of the variable being examined as the point for the symbol. Of course, dot-distribution mapping shows the density function directly and may be preferred to the center of gravity approach.

As in other research domains, in cartography, means and standard deviations are used as measures of central tendency and dispersion for interval data. Medians and decile range (e.g., between first and ninth deciles) are used for ordinal data. Modes and the variation ratio (fraction of cases not in the modal category) are used for nominal data.

Geographic Means. When aggregate values are to be averaged across geographic units of different size, it is conventional to weight each value by the size of its area if the value being studied is area related. This is the geographic mean. For county data on value of farmland per acre, for instance, one would multiply each county's value by its area, sum for all counties, and divide by the total area of all counties in the study. For variables that are not area related, such as income per capita, geographic means are not appropriate.

Location Quotients. Location quotients are commonly used to measure geographical shares of some phenomenon that are assumed to be uniformly distributed. For instance, for a given state one might compute the percentage of the total vote that was for the Democratic party, say, 45%. Then for each voting district the location quotient would be the ratio of that district's percentage Democratic to the state proportion (.45). Districts with location quotients greater than 1.0 would be more Democratic than the state as a whole, and those with quotients less than 1.0 would be less so. Note that as a ratio of percentages, the location quotient is independent of scale, which allows comparisons across maps of different types. Ranges of location quotients (e.g., < .9, .9 to 1.1, > 1.1) might be displayed in a choropleth map to highlight geographical shares. However, underrepresentation is compressed into the 0-1.0 range, while over-representation may take any value above 1.0. Together with the fact that the location quotient is very sensitive to the size and shape of the areas under study, many authors prefer to use standardized *z* scores rather than the location quotient for purposes of comparison on percentage ratios.

Centroid Computation. Atlas*GIS, IDRISI, and most other mapping pack-ages implement centroid computation. However, there are different types of centroids. The areal unit centroid is the center of an area with respect to its boundaries. The areal population centroid is the center of an area with respect to the distribution of its population. The weighted centroid is the center of an area with respect to the magnitudes on some attribute of a population distribution.

Areal unit centroids are computed by taking a series of representative points around the perimeter of an area, regardless of its shape. A list of the (x, y) coordinates of these points is made, with the last point having the same location as the first so as to close the polygon described by the points. As discussed by Griffith and Amrhein (1991, p. 116), the area of the polygon, A, and the coordinates of the areal unit centroid (x_c, y_c) can be computed from the following formulas, where k is the number of points and y_0 equals y_k:

$$A = \left| \sum_{i=1}^{k} x_i (y_{i+1} - y_{i-1})/2 \right|$$

The area is expressed in arbitrary units for purposes of the next two formulas for the x and y coordinates of the areal unit centroid:

58

$$x_c = \left| \sum_{i=1}^{k} (y_i - y_{i+1})(x_i^2 + x_i x_{i+1} + x_{i+1}^2) \right| / (6A)$$

$$y_c = \left| \sum_{i=1}^{k} (x_i - x_{i+1})(y_i^2 + y_i y_{i+1} + y_{i+1}^2) \right| / (6A)$$

The areal population centroid is also called the *population centroid* or the *spatial mean*. It is the statistic used when, after each decennial census, the Bureau of the Census announces which American community is the "geographic center of the United States." The population centroid is simply the mean longitude and latitude of the set of all population points. Often, however, the area is divided into sections and population is reported by section. While the coordinates of the areal unit centroids for the section are known, the coordinates for individual population points are not known. In this case the longitude ($\bar{x}$ in the equation below) of the center of a population of n observations in an area of s sections with n_i population each is computed as follows:

$$\bar{x} = \frac{\sum\limits_{i=1}^{s} n_i x_i}{N}$$

That is, one sums for all sections the product of the section population times the section longitude (using the section centroid), then averages by dividing by the total area population, N (Bachi, 1968, p. 107). The latitude of the center is computed the same way.

Weighted centroids are similar to areal population centroids, but weight each population point for its magnitude on some variable of interest. For instance, when the data are magnitudes rather than counts (e.g., income rather than population), the sections or points may be weighted differentially by magnitude of the variable being measured. Some authors call such weighted centroids the "center of gravity," while others assume weighting when discussing centroids for magnitude data. For point data, one simply multiplies point longitudes times point magnitudes, then sums for all points, then divides by the total of the point magnitudes. Latitudes would be computed in the same way. When data are reported by section rather than for individual points, one would multiply the section magnitude (e.g., mean income) times the section population times the section longitude, then average by dividing by the sum of the cross products of section populations and section magnitudes (e.g., mean incomes).

Naturally, the centroid will vary according to what is being measured. In a study of in-migration versus out-migration, for instance, each section will have a value for emigrants and a value for immigrants, and one may compute the geographic center for each of the two variables for purposes of comparison. Centrographic analysis is the study of the spatial changes in centroids over time, where centroids may reflect population, income, or other variables.

Spatial Median. The spatial median is the point in an area having the minimum distance to the areal unit centroids of all sections within the area (Griffith & Amrhein, 1991, p. 122). It is computed in an iterative fashion. Let U_0 and V_0 be the coordinates initially estimated as those of the spatial median. The initial estimate might be the coordinates of the population centroid. Then for t trials the U coordinate is reestimated using the following formula until an additional trial makes no significant difference:

$$U_t = \left\{ \sum_{i=1}^{n} f_i x_i / [(x_i - U_{t-1})^2 + (y_i - V_{t-1})^2]^{1/2} \right\} / \left\{ \sum_{i=1}^{n} f_i / [(x_i - U_{t-1})^2 + (y_i - V_{t-1})^2]^{1/2} \right\}$$

In this formula f_i is the frequency or population of the ith section. The V coordinate for the spatial median is computed in the same manner except that in the formula the first term after the first summation is $f_i y_i$ instead of $f_i x_i$.

Standard Distance. Standard distance is a measure of the average distance between points on a surface and, more specifically, of the dispersion of points about the areal population centroid (spatial mean). Thus it can be used in drawing contour lines about the spatial mean. Average interpoint distance can be computed as the mean, median, or mode, or as the mean quadratic distance (the square root of the mean of the squares of the distances). Standard distance, in contrast, can be calculated by computing the square root of the sum of the variances of the longitudes and latitudes of all points on the surface. This can be computed by the following formula:

$$d = \sqrt{ \left[\sum_{i=1}^{n} f_i (x_i - \bar{x})^2 / \sum_{i=1}^{n} f_i \right] - \left[\sum_{i=1}^{n} f_i (y_i - \bar{y})^2 / \sum_{i=1}^{n} f_i \right] }$$

In this formula, f_i is the frequency or population count in the ith of n units in the area under consideration. The x_i and y_i terms, of course, are the longitudes and latitudes of the data. The two terms in square brackets under the square root radical are the sums of the biased sample variances of the longitudes and latitudes (Bachi, 1968, p. 107; Griffith & Amrhein, 1991, p. 123). For larger samples, the bias does not matter. For smaller samples, one may substitute $(f_i - 1)$ for f_i in the denominator of each bracketed term. Standard distance is used in comparing the dispersion of different phenomena over a given surface, as in comparing the dispersion of different ethnic groups in a territory (see Bachi, 1968).

Proximity Pattern Measures. The most common proximity measure is probably average distance to the nearest neighbor, denoted as R (see Rogers, 1974, pp. 8-10). For a given point the nearest neighbor distance is, of course, just the distance to the nearest other point in the area. Often, however, the nearest neighbor statistic has a different meaning that applies to the set of all points in an area. For such summary purposes R is computed by the following formula:

$$R = 2\bar{d}\sqrt{(n/a)}$$

In this formula, $\bar{d}$ is the mean distance of each point to its nearest neighbor, n is the number of points in the area, and a is the size of the area. R will vary from 0 when all points are at the same location within the area to 1 when points are randomly distributed throughout the area. R will approach 2 as the points are uniformly distributed throughout an area in a nonrandom manner so as to maximize distances between points. The nearest neighbor statistic, therefore, can be used in point pattern analysis to assess the extent to which data are patterned, with 0 showing clustering, 2 showing uniform spacing, and 1 showing lack of pattern.

Dacey (1968) has shown for data on U.S. towns that nearest-larger neighbor data conform to the gamma distribution, which therefore may be the appropriate assumption in goodness-of-fit tests. If average nearest neighbor distance is interpreted as a measure of clustering, unusual data distributions may lead to misinterpretation, as in the case of closely paired points where the pairs are randomly distributed in the area. In that case, average nearest neighbor distance would approach zero but dispersion would be great. Also, R reflects boundary placement as well as point pattern. For the same pattern of points, R will shrink toward zero as the size of the area around the set of points becomes very large. Because of such problems, sometimes it may be appropriate to use an alternative proximity measure such as average interpoint distance or average distance to a fixed point (e.g., a feature centroid).[11]

Average spacing measures the mean distance between phenomena. It is computed as 1.0746 times the square root of the quantity, area units divided by number of phenomena. The distance, of course, will be expressed as linear units of the measure of area units. Thus, if there are 10 doctors in a 1,000 square-mile area, then the average spacing of doctors will be 1.0746 times the square root of (1000/10), which computes to be 10.746 miles.

There are a wide variety of other proximity measures that may be used for grouping points into regions. Leung (1988, chap. 3) has reviewed alternative approaches to grouping based on the concepts of similarity, distance, and the asymmetric spatial relations. Algorithms for proximity searching are detailed in Samet (1990).

Point Potential. Gravity models of spatial diffusion go back to Ravenstein's (1885-1889/1976) turn-of-the-century work *The Laws of Migration*.[12] They are based on the theory that exchanges between locations are proportional to the product of the size or mass (M) of the locations ($1, \ldots, n$) and inversely proportional to some exponent (x) of the distance (d) between them. As defined by astronomer J. Q. Stewart, the potential of any given point on a surface is defined as follows:

$$P_i = \sum_{j=1}^{n} (M_j/d_{ij}^x)$$

That is, the potential at any given surface point i is the sum from 1 to n total points, of the mass M of each other point j divided by the distance between i and j to the xth power. When x is 1, as is customary, each observation contributes to the total potential by an amount equal to the reciprocal of the distances from other points. For a given point with respect to another point, with x equal to 1, potential is the number of people in the given point divided by their distance from the second point.

The mean potential of all points on a surface is a measure of the likelihood of diffusion in a gravity model. Interactance (I) is defined differently but is an alternative measure of diffusion based on population size and per capita activity of two points (see Mackay, 1968). While gravity models are simplistic, they may provide a useful baseline of "expected diffusion" with which to compare observed diffusion. Potential of a point has been shown to be a good estimator of density of area around that point when area density data are unavailable (Stewart & Warntz, 1968, p. 139).

Note that the potentials of each point may be connected by isolines to show areas of equipotential propinquity and, as such, form a density map (see Stewart & Warntz, 1968, p. 137). If the mass (M in the equation) is not population number but a variable, such as number of persons who rate the president's foreign policy positively, then the isarithmic map becomes a mapping of political activity.

Breakpoint Measures. Summary statistics have also been devised for measuring the breakpoint between two socially defined features. For instance, Reilly's law of markets delimits a breakpoint between the trade areas of a pair of centers based on their size and spatial separation (Selkirk, 1982, pp. 96-98). This is used in determining "circles of attraction," "spheres of influence," or "preference areas." O'Kelly and Miller (1989) have generalized this model using probability contour mapping and numerical integration. These methods apply to any social interaction model for descriptive and predictive purposes.

Areal Correspondence. The coefficient of areal correspondence is a measure of the extent of congruence of two areas. For instance, one might have an isarithmic map showing the area covered by a certain level of investment in education and another map showing the area covered by a certain level of proportion of agricultural jobs in the work force. The coefficient of areal correspondence is simply the area covered jointly by both phenomena expressed as a percentage of the total area covered by both phenomena.

Network Measures. A network consists of a series of points, $P_1, \ldots, P_n$, connected by paths. The distance between any two points is the length of the shortest path connecting them. The associated number of a point is the maximum number of steps (i.e., number of point-to-point paths) from that point to any other point. The central point or central place in a network is the point with the lowest associated number. An associated number of 1, for instance, means you can get from that point to all others in one step, not passing through any other points. The diameter of a network is the maximum associated number.

The maximum number of routes (L^*) in a network connecting m points is $L^* = m(m - 1)/2$. The degree of connectivity in a network is L^*/r, where r is the observed number of routes. Connectivity will vary between the minimum (defined as $L^*/[m - 1]$) and the maximum connectivity (1.0) (see

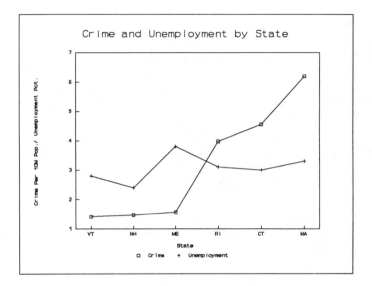

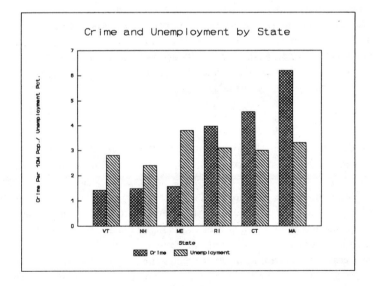

Figure 4.8. Geographic-Based Common Graphs

Garrison, 1968, p. 243). However, one might prefer the observed number of routes as a percentage of the maximum (L^*) as a measure of connectivity.

Dispersion in a network is the sum of all interpoint distances, including the distance from B to A as well as from A to B. Accessibility of a point in a network is the sum of distances from that point to all other points (Shimbel, 1953).

Network density refers to a methodology based on counting junctions and paths. First, a grid is overlaid on the map. Within each grid cell, junctions are points showing the intersection of roads or other paths in a network. The smallest junction has three paths: the first route path in to the point, the first route path out from the point, and the path out from the point of a route starting at that point. Assign a value of 1 to such smallest junctions; assign a 2 to junctions that are intersections of two routes; assign a 3 for junctions that are at points from which 5 routes emanate; and so on. For each cell in the grid, compute the sum of junction values. Connect cells with junction values in the same range with density contour lines. In this way network densities can become the basis for isopleth mapping in the analysis of transportation or other networks.

The alpha index of connectivity measures the completeness of a network as the percentage of circuits that are completed (Selkirk, 1982, pp. 164-166). The cyclomatic number, μ, is the number of completed circuits in an area. A completed circuit is a set of three or more paths connecting four or more points in which the first and last points are at the same location, such that a region is enclosed. Assuming a network with at least three points, the observed number of circuits, which is termed the *cyclomatic number*, can be computed by Euler's formula:

$$\mu = r - 1 = e - v + p,$$

where r is the number of regions into which the circuits divide an area (note the area outside the network is also counted as a region: a circle bisected with one path from point A to point B has three regions—the two semicircles and the area outside the circle), e is the number of edges (point-to-point paths), v is the number of vertices (number of points), and p is the number of unconnected networks in an area (normally 1; the number of unconnected networks is termed the *number of subgraphs*).

Assume a graph with no duplicate edges (i.e., no situation in which there is more than one path between two adjacent points). In planar graphs, which are networks that exist on a plane, draw edges such that the maximum number of regions are created but with the constraint that no edge cross another. For planar networks the maximum number of regions will be $2v - 4$. Therefore, since the number of circuits equals the number of regions minus 1 (since the external region is not a circuit), the maximum number of circuits is $2v - 5$. Thus the alpha index of connectivity is $\alpha = \mu/(2v - 5)$. Alpha is the ratio of observed completed circuits to the maximum possible.

Note, however, that for nonplanar networks the maximum number of circuits is much larger, since all vertices may be connected without the line-crossing constraint. In this case, $\alpha = \mu/[.5(v - 1)(v - 2)]$. There is also an alternative index of connectivity, β, whose formula is the same for both planar and nonplanar networks: $\beta = e/v$. This ratio of edges to vertices is easier to compute, but is less intuitive in meaning as a measure of connectivity and hence is less preferred.

Network paths can be represented in matrix form. The square matrix will have as many rows and columns as there are places in the network. Entries in the matrix are 1 if there is a direct path (not passing through other points) from a given place to another given place, and 0 if there is not. The diagonal, reflecting the inapplicability of paths from a given point to itself, is composed of 0s. A matrix with all 1s except the diagonal reflects a network with maximum connectivity (the maximum number of routes). A matrix with 1s immediately on either side of the diagonal but 0s everywhere else reflects a network with minimum connectivity (a single line through all points).

By matrix algebra, raising a network matrix X to the nth power computes how many ways a given point may be reached from another given point in n steps. That is, the entry x_{ij} will show how many ways one may reach point j from point i in n steps. If one computes this for one step, two steps, three steps, and so on until the nth matrix has no 0s, this nth matrix is the solution matrix. The matrix T, which is the sum of all these matrices from 1 to n steps, reflects the degree of connectivity in a network. The row and column totals of the T matrix are indicators of the accessibility of each place in the network (Shimbel, 1953). For additional reading on matrices, networks, and routing problems, see Selkirk (1982, chaps. 27-30) and Wilson and Kirkby (1980, chap. 4).

Quadrat Analysis. Quadrat analysis originated in the agricultural sciences in the early 1950s (Greig-Smith, 1952) as a method under which an area is divided into a grid with equal size cells called *quadrats*. The distribution of observations within each quadrat is then analyzed for variation from randomness. Quadrat analysis often uses the Poisson distribution, which is frequently taken as a data assumption in the study of uncommon events (e.g., plant disease in a field of mostly healthy plants). One computes the mean and variance of the observations in each quadrat.

Because the variance of the Poisson distribution is equal to its mean in the case of random distribution, the coefficient of variation (CV, the variance-mean ratio) will be 1 if the subject of study is randomly distributed over an area. To the extent the variance divided by the mean is greater than 1, the subject is clustered. To the extent the ratio is less than 1, the distribution is more regularly dispersed than would be expected at random (Rogers, 1974, p. 6). The difference between the variance-mean ratio and 1 has a standard error of the square root of $[2/(N-1)]$, where N is the number of observations. In using a t test with this standard error, the number of degrees of freedom is N minus 1. Alternatively, one may apply a chi-square goodness-of-fit test comparing actual observations with the number expected under Poisson distribution assumptions (Rogers, 1974, pp. 7-8). As Rogers (1974) has shown, the goodness-of-fit approach can use a variety of distribution assumptions to determine which provides the best fit to the data. For instance, in his study of retail trade, Rogers found that the negative binomial distribution provided the most satisfactory fit (p. 92). Of course, the same observed pattern of dispersion may be approximated by more than one underlying probability distribution.

Quadrat analysis is affected by the size of the grid used. A common rule of thumb is to set the grid interval width at the square root of the quantity two times area divided by n, the total number of observations. Quadrat analysis is also affected by the choice of center point over which the grid is located and the orientation of the grid (statistically, these should be set randomly). Finally, it is affected by the density of observations. For these reasons quadrat analysis is appropriate for the study of dispersion but not pattern. IDRISI is an example of a mapping package in which the statistics module supports quadrat analysis.

Spatial Autocorrelation. Spatial autocorrelation is the geostatistical extension of classical correlation and is defined as a measure of the degree of interdependence among areally distributed data in a plane (see Bennett, 1979, pp. 36, 490-493; Griffith & Amrhein, 1991, pp. 133-134). It is *auto*correlation because it deals with the correlation of values of a single variable that is due to their geographic arrangement, whereas Pearsonian correlation deals with the correlation of the paired values of two variables. When spatial autocorrelation is zero, the values under study are randomly distributed with respect to geography. When spatial autocorrelation approaches positive unity, similar values tend to cluster at the same location. When spatial autocorrelation approaches negative unity, dissimilar values tend to cluster at the same location.

The first step in computing spatial autocorrelation is to construct a configuration table. This is a table in which both the rows and the columns list the sections into which the area is divided. Entries in the cells of the configuration table are 1 if the row and column sections share a geographical boundary, 0 if they do not. (Refinements exist for more complex algorithms that reflect the extent to which two sections share a boundary.) This configuration table is n by n in size with n_2 cells, which we may label c_{ij}, where i is the row and j is the column of the cell. A zero is entered for all cells on the main diagonal (where $i = j$).

Procedure after construction of the configuration table differs depending on the level of data. For nominal data the join count statistic is used, whereas for interval data the Moran coefficient or the Geary ratio is used. The join ratio statistic requires coding each section with a 1 if a given variable is present, 0 if it is not. On the analogy of a game board on which white squares indicate presence of the variable (1) and black squares indicate its absence (0), let WW equal the number of adjacent sections (pairs coded 1 on one triangle of the configuration table—one triangle so as not to double-count the A-B and B-A border, for instance) that are both coded 1 on the variable; let BB = the number of adjacent sections both coded 0 on the variable; and let BW equal the number of adjacent sections coded differently on the variable. W, B, and BW are the observed spatial autocorrelation statistics, also called the *join count statistics*.

The next step in spatial autocorrelation is to compute the expected values of WW, BB, and BW. The expected values are the values anticipated when no spatial autocorrelation is present. Let $J = $ WW + BB +BW, which is the sum of pairs of adjacent sections, which is the sum of the 1s entered in one triangle of the configuration table. Let n_1 equal the number of sections coded 1 on the variable and let n_2 equal the number of units coded 0. Then the expected values are as follows (Griffith & Amrhein, 1991, p. 136):

$$E(WW) = Jn_1(n_1 - 1)/[n(n - 1)]$$

$$E(BB) = Jn_2(n_2 - 1)/[n(n - 1)]$$

$$E(BW) = 2Jn_1n_2/[n(n - 1)]$$

Note that E(BW) is multiplied by 2 because W pairs include 0-1 as well as 1-0 variable code pairs. The WW, BB, and BW observed spatial autocorrelation statistics can be compared with their corresponding expected values. The closer the observed and expected values, the stronger the conclusion that the spatial distribution of the variable is geographically random.

For interval data one may use the Moran coefficient (MC) or the Geary ratio (GR) as measures of spatial autocorrelation. MC has the following formula based on cross products of deviations from the mean of the variable under study for pairs of juxtaposed sections:

$$MC = \left(n \Big/ \sum_{i=1}^{n} \sum_{j=1}^{n} c_{ij} \right) \left[\sum_{i=1}^{n} \sum_{j=1}^{n} c_{ij}(x_i - \bar{x})(x_j - \bar{x}) \Big/ \sum_{i=1}^{n} (x_i - \bar{x})^2 \right]$$

In this formula the c_{ij}s are the entries in the configuration table, the x_is and x_js are the observed values of the variable for the i and j juxtaposed areal sections. MC is computed in a manner analogous to Pearson's r and, with exceptions, varies between -1 and $+1$. Positive unity means like values cluster and negative unity means dissimilar values tend to cluster; 0 indicates that values are randomly scattered geographically.

The Geary ratio is based on paired comparisons of values in adjacent sections. The formula is as follows:

$$GR = \left((n-1) \Big/ 2 \sum_{j=1}^{n} \sum_{i=1}^{n} c_{ij} \right) \left[\sum_{j=1}^{n} \sum_{i=1}^{n} c_{ij}(x_i - x_j)^2 \Big/ \sum_{i=1}^{n} (x_i - \bar{x})^2 \right]$$

With exceptions, GR ranges from 0 to 2. GR is 0 when similar values tend to cluster, 2 when dissimilar values cluster, and 1 when random scattering is indicated. Thus as R goes up, MC will go down. Because of differences in the formulas, however, the two measures are not always interchangeable on an inverse basis.

Spatial autoregression is an extension involving use of time lags of the dependent variable as independent variables in a regression model (Bennett, 1979, pp. 40-41, 153-154). IDRISI is an example of a package in which the statistics module implements single- and multiple-lag autocorrelation, based on Moran's I statistic. This is the version preferred for interval scaled data; a rank version is available (Cliff, 1973; Cliff & Ord, 1975; Moran, 1950).

Autocorrelation is used in selection of area sampling methods. When geographic autocorrelation declines monotonically with distance, systematic (interval) sampling has been found to be efficient. When the shape of the autocorrelation function is unknown, stratified random areal sampling is recommended (Berry & Baker, 1968, p. 98). Also, space-time cross-correlation combines use of time lags with space lags to apply autocorrelation and autoregression methods to the study of diffusion problems, as in epidemiology (see Bennett, 1979, pp. 490-499).

Trend Surface Analysis. Trend surface mapping is an extension of multiple regression that attempts to model isarithmic maps using a variety of functions. Where control points in regular isarithmic maps are taken "as is" to plot contour lines, trend surface analyses attempt to create more complex models for the purpose of simplifying presentation to highlight trends. A simple example is the use of moving averages of sets of control points rather than individual control point data to smooth isarithmic lines. Another simple example, described by Mather (1991, pp. 93-97), uses longitude and latitude coordinates as independent variables in linear regression to predict a dependent variable (e.g., pollution level). Predictions are then associated with categorical ranges of the dependent variable and plotted to show isometric patterns.

More complex quadratic (see Mather, 1991, pp. 97-98), cubic, and quartic transformations can create smoothing effects reflective of more complex surfaces (Chorley & Haggett, 1968). An isarithmic pattern characterized by one dome or one trough may be modeled by a second-order trend surface in which the regression model includes x^2, xy, and y^2 terms in addition to the x and y coordinates of the areal unit centroids and the intercept (constant). Third-order trend surfaces model isarithms with a hill and valley with one inflection point each. This regression model requires all the terms of second-order regressions plus x^3, x^2y, xy^2, and y^3 terms. Fourth-order or higher models for wavy surfaces are rare in the literature.

Multicollinearity is reduced in trend surface analysis through conversion of data to standardized z scores. Other transforms, such as Fourier transforms, are appropriate to smoothing and estimation where surfaces exhibit cyclical or rippling effects or other noise (Harbaugh & Preston, 1968). Like other forms of analysis using isarithms, an assumption of trend surface analysis is that the spatial distribution of the variable of interest is continuous over the area in question. Also, trend surface mapping assumes an uncorrelated coordinate system, but when centroid coordinates are used as predictor variables, this assumption is violated, especially when the centroids are not spaced in a regular grid pattern. IDRISI's statistics module supports formulation of third-order trend surfaces. For an introduction to trend surface models, see Griffith and Amrhein (1991, chap. 15).

Tessellation. While not a form of statistical analysis per se, tessellation lays related groundwork. Tessellation is the division of a plane into cells that partition the whole. That is, tessellation divides an area into a set of arbitrary subareas for purposes of spatial analysis. Tessellation is particularly appropriate when analyzing a large surface that is not divided by accepted natural or social internal boundaries. Square cells are most common, but some models use triangles, hexagons, and other polygons. For instance, tessellation is used in archaeology during the planning of excavations. Imposition of a grid over an area is a form of tessellation, although tessellation methods can be considerably more complex, particularly in analysis of three-dimensional objects.[13] For instance, Dirichlet tessellation subdivides an area such that each point within that area has associated with it a polygon defining a region nearer to that point than to any other. In ecological studies Dirichlet tessellations are used to establish the "area potentially available" to an individual point (e.g., a tree) in a population. Further mathematical wrinkles of tessellation deal with edge effects, where it is desirable to exclude from analysis all polygons that are potentially influenced by individuals located outside the mapped study area (Kenkel, Hoskins, & Hoskins, 1989). For more on optimization of tesseral addressing schemes and quality measures for evaluating alternatives, see Taylor (1986). IDRISI's statistics module is an example of software that supports shape analysis and Thiessen tessellation.

GEOGRAPHIC GRAPHS AND PLOTS

Many of the statistics common in social science generally are applicable in relation to cartography as well. For instance, one could use regression residuals for values where control points were towns, then plot an isarithmic map showing areas of unexplained variation in the dependent variable (see Haggett, 1968, p. 323; Thomas, 1968). On correlation and regression, see Robinson, Lindberg, and Brinkman (1968). On factor analysis, see Wong (1968). For a general discussion of application of conventional statistical techniques to mapping, see Dickinson (1963).

Geographic line, area, scatterplot, bar, and pie charts are among the many ways of analyzing geographic data. Such charting is built into many GIS packages (e.g., MapInfo and MapInfo for Windows), although it can be accomplished using generic packages such as spreadsheets since no actual map is involved. Even clip art mapping packages such as MapArt allow pasting of bar charts onto corresponding map areas for visual effect. Figure 4.8 illustrates use of geographic data in common line and bar graphs. The illustration used is crime rate per 10 million population and unemployment percentage, by state.

Although the geographic units in Figure 4.8 are states ordered by crime rate, they could just as well be cities ordered by population or census blocks ordered by percentage nonwhite. This form of analytic graphics is so basic that it almost needs no mention, but we illustrate it here because social scientists are prone to equate common graphs with use of numeric variables alone.

Geographic graphs are merely one instance of many applications that use geographic-related data for conventional statistical analysis (for more on graphic presentation, see Cleveland & McGill, 1988; Holmes, 1984; Meilach, 1990; Robertson, 1988; Sutton, 1988; Tufte, 1983; Zelazny, 1985). Other examples include such software as the Economic Analysis System (Essential Solutions, Springfield, MO) for economic base and shift share analysis, the Community Analysis and Planning Programs from the University of Akron (see Klosterman, 1989), and County Business Patterns Analysis for analysis of census CBP data (National Collegiate Software, Duke University Press, Durham, NC).

CUSTOM ANALYSIS

Some GIS packages contain built-in programming languages that allow users to go beyond standard analytic features. MapInfo, for example, contains the MapCode programming language, which is a macro language. Macro languages allow users to record series of commands as a batch file, then execute them all at once. For instance, a macro could be created to select automatically all datapoints meeting some proximity criterion, then display them on a map with a certain scale and set of overlays, all of this activated by a new user-defined menu item or special (e.g., Alt or Function) keystroke. MapCode also allows calling up external applications, such as faxing map output automatically. Likewise, Atlas*GIS supports the ATLAS* SCRIPT optional module for creating custom applications. GisPlus is a microcomputer GIS package noted for its flexibility in creating custom applications.

5. PRESENTATION

Output Issues

Many printers support control languages that allow manipulation of maps as well as other graphic images. For instance, the HP LaserJet supports PCL (Printer Control Language; enhanced in the LaserJet III version) for printing text, and HPGL (Hewlett Packard Graphics Language) for line drawing and plotting.

Mapping software packages take advantage of printer capacities (e.g., the capacity to support PostScript desktop publishing). Indeed, selection of mapping software depends in no small part on what hardware it can be installed for. To illustrate a common configuration, one might have a Macintosh II computer with a PostScript laser printer and a 300 dpi (dots per inch) scanner for input purposes. Although Macintosh-based software (e.g., Atlas*Pro for Macintosh) has traditionally had an edge in computer-aided presentation graphics, new Windows-based software now provides a competitive alternative (e.g., ATLAS*MapMaker for Windows, MapInfo for Windows).

The ability of GIS to bridge the gap between serious data management and top-quality presentation is a unique strength. Laser printers are a common and affordable means of producing high-quality thematic output of GIS product. Most packages will support laser-printed output in either HPGL or PostScript formats. Industry standards are gravitating toward PostScript for its cleaner lines and curve-drawing ability.

The limitations of laser-printed output within the context of GIS are precision and affordable color. Whereas laser printers offer 300 dpi output, pen plotters "move in steps of about 0.001 inch—more than three times finer than typical laser engines" (Rosch, 1990, p. 134). In addition, pen plotters offer inexpensive color that is vital to clear understanding of complex map hatching. Pen plotters can also utilize a variety of media at either 8.5 × 11- or 11 × 17-inch sizes. While freestanding plotters require significant expenditures, desktop models can be acquired for prices comparable to laser printers. Desktop models should be suitable for most social science applications; however, for larger-format output many blueprinting and surveying services are able to create large-size plots from files in common formats (.DXF, for example) received by modem.

· Desktop publishing for many researchers is the "bottom line" of mapping. Leading presentation-quality desktop publishing and graphics packages such as Harvard Graphics recognize this in their product line. Harvard GeoGraphics (a successor to Harvard Graphics MapMaker Accessory) is an example. It offers four map libraries (world countries, U.S. states, U.S. counties, and aggregate three-digit ZIP code areas) as well as an extensive point database of cities (60,000 U.S.; 3,000 international). Choropleth maps can be created by linking Harvard GeoGraphics to data in Lotus 1-2-3 or ASCII formats. Maps support the .SYM, .CHT, .EPS, .HPGL, .CGM, and .PCX file formats. Users can customize maps with text callouts, city icons, titles, symbol library images, and map legends. Maps can be rotated, moved, copied, sized, and edited.

Desktop publishing and graphics packages such as Harvard GeoGraphics are not full GIS systems and do not allow advanced geographic analysis work. However, it is often possible to import maps from GIS packages into software such as Harvard GeoGraphics and then take advantage of its superior handling of fonts, images, shading, and other desktop publishing features. Many publishers offer a series of presentation mapping packages covering a spectrum of capabilities. For instance, Strategic Mapping's low-end product is ATLAS*MapMaker, which supports spreadsheet data entry and simple presentation mapping. Its mid-level product is Atlas*Pro, for Macintosh or MS-DOS. Atlas*Pro comes with an extensive database manager and has extensive map layout tools for custom design of a wide variety of presentation maps. Strategic Mapping's high-end package is Atlas*GIS, a desktop geographic information system with sophisticated overlay, map digitizing, spatial analysis, and other advanced features.

Display Issues

Most GIS packages have display needs similar to desktop publishing programs and other applications that have intensive screen drawing operations. Minimum requirements of an EGA or VGA monitor for map display are the standard, but requirements do vary. For instance, LandTrak 3.44 requires an additional monochrome text monitor. Also, the growing popularity and availability of 16- and 17-inch diagonal monitors is noteworthy to the context of desktop mapping. Overall system performance will depend in large part on display speed. A math coprocessor and a display card with abundant RAM will provide the performance necessary to make the most of GIS.

Graphic Misrepresentation Issues

The data on which maps are based are subject to measurement error (bad data), errors of aggregation (wrongly combined data), and errors of computation (wrong formulas). As Klosterman (1990) has noted:

> Easy-to-use tools for spreadsheet modeling, database management, and statistical analysis and forecasting allow planning professionals to develop models and prepare analyses that were once the unique domain of academics and large regional agencies. However, with this new capability comes the potential for building and using models that are poorly conceived, improperly documented, and computationally incorrect. (pp. 180-181)

One author has popularized these concerns in a book titled *How to Lie With Maps* (Monmonier, 1991).

Establishment of geographic association between two variables, as by overlaying two maps to show geographic coincidence of disease occurrence and a disease factor, does not establish causation. The factor may not cause the disease, even if geographically coincidental. Thus, while geographic analysis may be particularly revealing and may provoke causal hypotheses for further explanation, it is not a substitute for standard multivariate techniques (e.g., MLGH techniques such as regression and analysis of variance models) used to unravel complex causal interdependencies (see Matthews, 1990, p. 217).

Choropleth and even isopleth maps may be misinterpreted easily to suggest that all points are equal within a given feature (area) in a choropleth map or within a given contour line in an isopleth map. That is, choropleth maps can be misleading when used to represent magnitude, because people tend to confuse this with density. Thus a small urban county of 100,000 population and a much larger county of 100,000 population would both be colored the same shade (or pattern or color) on a choropleth map of population sizes. Some would interpret this as meaning population density is the same in both counties. In contrast, a circle-distribution map would show same-size circles in each county, but in the larger county the circle would be a smaller portion of the total map area; in choropleth mapping the shaded area would be all of the map areas of both counties (Monmonier, 1991, p. 23).

As Southall and Oliver (1990) note, an assumption of equality based on choropleth maps is "obviously true of altitude above sea level, or air temperature, but is less likely to be true of data about human affairs; for example, can we talk about average income where there are no people . . . ?"

(p. 147). Moreover, when data are sparse, as is often the case in social science, results can be particularly misleading. In general, data cannot be properly interpreted without knowledge of the underlying distribution of the population being mapped.

Likewise, it is essential to use the proper base when employing the geostatistics discussed in the preceding chapter. Area-linked variables such as trees, pollutants, or people may be analyzed for dispersion/clustering on the basis of area, for instance, but vehicles must be analyzed on the basis of roads and traffic lights on the basis of intersections, not total area (Cole & King, 1968, p. 183).

Because color is more visually appealing, it is often used in spite of analytical shortcomings. When using color in choropleth maps, one should keep in mind that about 10% of the population is color-blind and may not be able to differentiate, say, green and red. Also, only a limited number of color gradations are easily perceived by the human eye. Therefore, hatch patterns or a limited number of gray scales may be more easily read by one's audience. Even with gray scales, empirical research has shown that map users overestimate low values and underestimate high values (Jenks & Knos, 1961).

In distribution maps that use symbols of differing size to show amounts (e.g., population size), the logical rule is to make the area of the symbol directly proportional to the amount being depicted. Unfortunately, it has been found that people consistently underestimate the amounts associated with larger symbols. Therefore, it may be advisable to increase the areas of symbols more than proportional to the amounts they represent. However, this makes it all the more important to have a clear and easily readable legend that shows the correspondence of symbols to amounts.

6. CONCLUSION

If a social science graduate student were to attend the annual computer expositions sponsored by *Government Computer News* and other organizations in Washington each year, or visit the annual meetings of the Urban and Regional Information Systems Association, some conclusions would be strikingly self-evident. First, geographic information systems constitute a billion-dollar business, not an obscure methodological sidelight. Second, GIS infuses every aspect of local, state, and federal government, from criminal justice to environmental administration to education. And third,

GIS is premised as part of decision support systems for top policymakers throughout government. As one tours such meetings one also finds booths for vendors of statistical packages, to be sure, but these are dwarfed by GIS applications. Attending such a meeting, the average social science graduate student will begin to wonder about the relevance of his or her research methods training to the real world of policy decisions.

Of course, the preceding paragraph oversells the point. There is no need to trade off statistical and GIS approaches one against the other when in fact they are complementary. It would be difficult to fit GIS into already-crowded research methods courses. This is particularly so because it embraces a new world of vocabulary and perspectives different from the language of multiple linear general hypotheses and the like. The social sciences, like social entities in general, deal with the growth of knowledge through specialization and differentiation, not integration. Still, there is a need for generalist knowledge that at least takes note of all the tools in the tool bag and comprehends what each can do even if mastery is achieved for only some of the tools.

The relation of the social sciences to GIS need not be a one-way street. There is a tendency of GIS to be business driven and to emphasize mapping as a visual aid rather than as a method of analysis. Most GIS software packages neglect geographic statistics such as measures discussed in this monograph. Social scientists have much to offer in the refinement of the techniques of analytic mapping. At the same time, as expert systems and artificial intelligence are used increasingly in GIS to automate pattern recognition, the field of analytic mapping provides social scientists with compelling alternatives to sole reliance on conventional multivariate statistical procedures.

APPENDIX: PRODUCTS MENTIONED

Arc/Info, Environmental Systems Research, Inc., 380 New York Street, Redlands, CA 92373; (714) 793-2853.

Atlas*GIS, Atlas*Pro, and ATLAS*MapMaker, Strategic Mapping, Inc., 4030 Moorpark Avenue, Suite 250, San Jose, CA 95117-1848; (408) 985-7400; fax (408) 985-0859.

AutoCAD, Autodesk Inc., 2320 Marinship Way, Sausalito, CA 94965; (415) 332-2344; (800) 443-0100.

Census Windows: TIGER Tools, GeoVision, Inc., 5680 B Peachtree Parkway, Norcross, GA 30092; (404) 448-8224; fax (404) 447-4565.

Compton's Multimedia Encyclopedia, Encyclopedia Britannica Educational Corp., 310 S. Michigan Avenue, Chicago, IL 60604; (800) 554-9862.

Elections, David L. Martin, 727 Wrights Mill Road, Auburn, AL 36830; (205) 821-0030 (evenings).

Equalizer, National Collegiate Software, Duke University Press. (In 1991, NCS became part of William C. Brown Publishers, Software Division, 2460 Kerper Boulevard, Dubuque, IA 52001.)

FMS/AC (Facilities Mapping System for AutoCAD), Facility Mapping Systems, Inc., 38 Miller Avenue, Suite 11, Mill Valley, CA 94941; (415) 381-1750; (800) 442-3674.

GEOdisc U.S. Atlas, GeoVision, Inc., 5680 B Peachtree Parkway, Norcross, GA 30092; (404) 448-8224; fax (404) 447-4565.

GIS/AMS, GeoVision, Inc., 5680 B Peachtree Parkway, Norcross, GA 30092; (404) 448-8224; fax (404) 447-4565.

Gis-Plus Geographic Information System, Caliper Corp.

Harvard GeoGraphics, Software Publishing Corp., 1901 Landings Drive, Mountain View, CA 94043; (415) 962-8910.

HiJaak, Inset Systems, Brookfield, CT.

IDRISI, c/o J. Ronald Eastman, Graduate School of Geography, Clark University, Worcester, MA 01610; (617) 793-7336.

AUTHORS' NOTE: Due to space limitations, a second appendix listing non-software GIS resources has been omitted. To obtain a copy, send a stamped, self-addressed manila envelope to G. David Garson, NCSU Box 8101, Raleigh, NC 27695-8101.

LandTrak, Geo-based Systems, 4800 Six Forks Road, Raleigh, NC 27609; (919) 783-8000.

MapAnalyst, National Planning Data Corporation, P.O. Box 610, Ithaca, NY 14851-0610; (800) 876-6732; (607) 273-8208; fax (607) 273-1266.

MapArt, Micromaps Software, 9 Church Street, P.O. Box 757, Lambertville, NJ 08530; (800) 334-4291; (609) 397-1611; fax (609) 397-5724.

MapInfo and RealTime MapInfo, Mapping Information Systems Corporation, 200 Broadway, Troy, NY 12180; (800) FAST-MAP; (518) 274-8673; fax (518) 274-0510.

MAX^{3d} Online Service Communications Software, National Planning Data Corporation, P.O. Box 610, Ithaca, NY 14851-0610; (800) 876-6732; (607) 273-8208.

PC CAD Interface: TIGER to DXF Conversion Utility, GeoVision, Inc., 5680 B Peachtree Parkway, Norcross, GA 30092; (404) 448-8224; fax (404) 447-4565.

PC Datagraphics and Mapping, National Collegiate Software, Duke University Press. (In 1991 NCS became part of William C. Brown Publishers, Software Division, 2460 Kerper Boulevard, Dubuque, IA 52001.)

PC Globe, PC Globe Inc., 4700 S. McClintock, Suite 150, Tempe, AZ 85282; (800) 255-2789.

PC-Key-Draw, OEDware, P.O. Box 595, Columbia, MD 21045-0595; (301) 997-9333.

Roots, Laboratory for Computer Graphics and Spatial Analysis, Graduate School of Design, Harvard University, 48 Quincy Street, Cambridge, MA 02138; (617) 495-2526.

SPSS Categories for Conjoint and Correspondence Analysis, SPSS Inc., 444 N. Michigan Avenue, Chicago, IL 60611; (312) 329-3300.

Surfer, Golden Software Inc., 807 14th Street, Box 281, Golden, CO 80402; (303) 279-1021.

Systat/Sygraph, Systat, Inc., 1800 Sherman Avenue, Evanston, IL 60201; (708) 864-5670; fax (708) 492-3567.

Time Magazine Compact Almanac, Compact Publishing, 4958 Ashby Street NW, Washington, DC 20007; (202) 244-4770.

Tralaine, American Digital Cartography, 715 West Parkway Boulevard, Appleton, WI 54914; (414) 733-6678; fax (414) 734-3375.

Trimble GPS, TrimbleNavigation, Attn. Ray Hiller, Building 5, Survey and Mapping Division, P.O. Box 3642, Sunnyvale, CA 94088-3642; (800) TRIMBLE.

U.S. Atlas, Software Toolworks Inc., 13557 Ventura Boulevard, One Todworks Plaza, Sherman Oaks, CA 91423; (818) 986-4885.

Windows/On the World, GeoVision, Inc., 5680 B Peachtree Parkway, Norcross, GA 30092; (404) 448-8224; fax (404) 447-4565.

World Atlas, Software Toolworks Inc., 13557 Ventura Boulevard, One Todworks Plaza, Sherman Oaks, CA 91423; (818) 986-4885.

World Projection and Mapping System, Social Science Research Facilities Center, University of Minnesota, Minneapolis, MN 55455; (612) 625-8556.

ZIP/Clip, Effective Data Solutions, 28030 Dorothy Drive, Suite 302, Agoura Hills, CA 91301; (800) 777-8818; (818) 991-3282.

ZipView, distributed by the Bureau of Electronic Publishing; (800) 828-4766.

NOTES

1. Seriation studies used for archaeological dating have usually been validated by later objective approaches, such as hydration studies. See Hatch, Michels, Stevenson, Scheetz, and Geidel (1990).

2. Control points are defined and discussed in the section on digitizing maps in Chapter 3. They are the coordinates used to connect contour lines in isopleth maps or to locate symbols in distribution maps.

3. Information about how to obtain this catalog and other useful resources mentioned in this monograph is available from the authors. Send a self-addressed stamped envelope to G. David Garson, College of Humanities and Social Science, 106 Caldwell, Hillsborough Street, North Carolina State University, Raleigh, NC 27695.

4. National Planning Data Corporation, P.O. Box 610, Ithaca, NY 14851-0610; (800) 876-6732; (608) 273-6732.

5. American Digital Cartography, 715 W. Parkway Boulevard, Appleton, WI 54914; (414) 733-6678; fax (414) 734-3375. As of 1991, a 60-square-mile map was priced at $200, with roads, terrain contours, and the like extra.

6. Cost for high-density 3.5-inch disks for personal computer CAD systems in 1991 was $55 per quadrangle, exclusive of options such as TIGER street names ($100), TIGER political boundaries ($100), TIGER names and boundaries ($125), and so on. Also, 1:2 MDLG state maps were available for $195 per state. See note 5 for ADC's address and phone numbers.

7. The GVF test is computed as follows. First, compute the sum of squared deviations of each value in the array from the array mean (SDAM, the squared deviations from the array mean). Second, divide the array into proposed classes and do the same thing for each class value for its class mean, and then sum all these to get the grand sum of squared deviations from the class means (SDCM). The GVF value is then (SDAM − SDCM)/ SDAM. One then tries other classifications through various iterations until one is satisfied that the GVF value is maximized. This will correspond to the classification for which the SDCM value is minimized, which is the classification with the lowest within-class variance.

8. Lavin and Archer (1984), of the University of Nebraska—Lincoln, also discuss BICHOR, a computer program for the generation of UBC maps.

9. We are indebted to an anonymous reviewer of an earlier version of the manuscript for observations in this paragraph. Moreover, there is reason to believe that the data used for control points for the isopleths shown in Figure 4.5 may be in error. For instance, 1981 data for Botswana and Angola show the latter to have more than twice the infant mortality of the former, whereas the figure shows the two countries to be similar.

10. These map types are defined and discussed in the first section of this chapter. Choropleth maps, the most common type used by social scientists, show the world, a country, or a region divided into political units that are colored or shaded according to the quantity or proportion of some variable associated with them. See Figure 4.2.

11. A feature centroid is the centroid of the smallest ellipse that can contain the feature.

12. This is reprinted in Ravenstein (1885-1889/1976). Ravenstein proposed certain mathematical "laws of migration" based on analysis of data from the 1881 census of the British Isles. For a review of Ravenstein's early immigration studies and related classic work, see Passaris (1989). For recent work building on (and mostly supportive of) Ravenstein's principles, see Arizpe (1978), Cole (1989), Dorigo and Tobler (1983), Hawrylyshyn (1977), Rootman (1988), Saunders (1983), and Wareing (1981).

13. For instance, in computer visualization three-dimensional conics can be used to approximate a model of objects in the environment. Intersection of the conics employs algorithms from computational geometry. Specifically, contour models are generated through tessellation (see Srinivasan, 1990).

REFERENCES

ANTES, J. R., and CHANG, K. (1990) "An empirical analysis of the design principles for quantitative and qualitative area symbols." Cartography and Geographic Information Systems 17(4): 271-277.

ARDALAN, N. (1988) "A dynamic archival system (DAS) for the clean-up of Boston harbor." URISA 1988 2: 97-103.

ARIZPE, L. (1978) "Migrant women and rural economy: Analysis of a migratory cohort to Mexico City, 1940-1970." America Indigena 38(2): 303-326.

ARMSTRONG, M. P. (1990) "Database integration for knowledge based groundwater quality assessment." Computers, Environment, and Urban Systems 14(3): 187-201.

ARMSTRONG, M. P., DENSHAM, P. J., and RUSHTON, G. (1986) "Architecture for a microcomputer based spatial decision support system," pp. 120-131 in Proceedings of the Second International Symposium on Spatial Data Handling. Williamsville, NY: International Geographical Union.

ARMSTRONG, M. P., RUSHTON, G., HONEY, R., DALZIEL, B., LOLONIS, P., DE, S., and DENSHAM, P. J. (1991) "Decision support for regionalization: A spatial decision support system for regionalizing service delivery systems." Computers, Environment, and Urban Systems 15(1-2): 37-53.

ASPAAS, H. R., and LAVIN, S. J. (1989) "Legend designs for unclassed, bivariate, choropleth maps." American Cartographer 16(4): 257-268.

BACHI, R. (1968) "Statistical analysis of geographical series," pp. 101-109 in B. J. L. Berry and D. F. Marble (eds.) Spatial Analysis: A Reader in Statistical Geography. Englewood Cliffs, NJ: Prentice-Hall.

BECKMANN, M. J., and PUU, T. (1985) Spatial Economics: Density, Potential, and Flow. New York: North-Holland.

BECKMANN, M. J., and PUU, T. (1990) Spatial Structures. New York: Springer-Verlag.

BENNETT, R. J. (1979) Spatial Time Series: Analysis—Forecasting—Control. London: Pion.

BERRY, B. J. L., and BAKER, A. M. (1968) "Geographic sampling," pp. 91-100 in B. J. L. Berry and D. F. Marble (eds.) Spatial Analysis: A Reader in Statistical Geography. Englewood Cliffs, NJ: Prentice-Hall.

BISHTON, A. (1988) "Designing and using a cartographic extract: Mapping from the TIGER system." URISA 1988 2: 130-141.

BOSSLER, J. D., FINNIE, T. C., PETCHENIK, B. B., and MUSSELMAN, T. M. (1990) "Spatial data needs: The future of the national mapping program." Cartography and Geographic Information Systems 17(3): 237-242.

BREWER, C. A. (1989) "The development of process-printed Munsell charts for selecting map colors." American Cartographer 16(4): 269-278.

BUNGE, W. (1962) Theoretical Geography. Lund, Sweden: C. W. K. Gleerup.

CHANDRA, N., and GORAN, W. (1986) "Steps toward a knowledge-based geographical data analysis system," pp. 749-764 in B. Opitz (ed.) Geographic Information Systems in Government. Hampton, VA: A. Deepak.

CHANG, K. (1980) "Circle size judgment and map design." American Cartographer 7: 155-162.

CHORLEY, R. J., and HAGGETT, P. (1968) "Trend-surface mapping in geographical research," pp. 195-217 in B. J. L. Berry and D. F. Marble (eds.) Spatial Analysis: A Reader in Statistical Geography. Englewood Cliffs, NJ: Prentice-Hall.

CLEVELAND, W. S., and McGILL, M. E. (eds.) (1988) Dynamic Graphics for Statistics. Belmont, CA: Wadsworth.

CLIFF, A. D. (1973) Spatial Autocorrelation. London: Pion.

CLIFF, A. D., and ORD, J. K. (1975) "The choice of a test for spatial autocorrelation," pp. 54-77 in J. C. Davis and M. J. McCullagh (eds.) Display and Analysis of Spatial Data. New York: John Wiley.

COLE, J. (1989) "Internal migration in Peru." Geography Review 3(1): 25-31.

COLE, J. P., and KING, C. A. M. (1968) Quantitative Geography. New York: John Wiley.

COTTER, D. M., and CAMPBELL, R. K. (1987) "Concept for a digital flood hazard data base." URISA 1987 2: 156-170.

CUFF, D. J., and MATTSON, M. T. (1982) Thematic Maps: Their Design and Production. New York: Routledge.

DACEY, M. F. (1968) "A family of density functions for Lösch's measurements on town distribution," pp. 168-171 in B. J. L. Berry and D. F. Marble (eds.) Spatial Analysis: A Reader in Statistical Geography. Englewood Cliffs, NJ: Prentice-Hall.

DANGERMOND, J. (1989) "A review of digital data commonly available and some of the practical problems of entering them into a GIS," in W. J. Ripple (ed.) Fundamentals of Geographic Information Systems: A Compendium. Bethesda, MD: American Society for Photogrammetry and Remote Sensing and the American Congress on Surveying and Mapping.

DARLING, C. B. (1991) "Waiting for distributed database." DBMS 4(10): 46-53.

DENSHAM, P. J., and GOODCHILD, M. (1989) "Spatial decision support systems: A research agenda," pp. 707-716 in Proceedings, GIS.LIS '89. Bethesda, MD: American Congress on Surveying and Mapping.

DENSHAM, P. J., and RUSHTON, G. (1988) "Decision support systems for locational planning," pp. 56-90 in R. G. Gollege and H. Timmermans (eds.) Behavioural Modelling in Geography and Planning. London: Croom Helm.

DENT, B. D. (1990) Cartography: Thematic Map Design (2nd ed.). Dubuque, IA: William C. Brown.

DICKINSON, G. C. (1963) Statistical Mapping and the Presentation of Statistics. London: Edward Arnold.

DIJKSTRA, E. W. (1959) "A note on two problems in connection with graphs." Numerische Mathematik 1: 269-271.

DORIGO, G., and TOBLER, W. (1983) "Push-pull migration laws." Annals of the Association of American Geographers 73(11): 1-17.

DUTT, A. K., KENDRICK, F. J., and NASH, T. (1979) "Areal variation in the 1976 presidential vote: A case study of Akron." Ohio Journal of Science 79(3): 120-125.

FIRESTONE, L. M. (1987) "Geographic processing of census data for earthquake loss-risk assessment in Utah." URISA 1987 2: 144-155.

FISHER, W. D. (1958) "On grouping for maximum homogeneity." Journal of the American Statistical Association 53: 789-798.

FITTS, A. M. (1989) "Words of the black belt and beyond: A study of Alabama lexical patterns in the 'Linguistic Atlas of the Gulf States.' " Dissertation Abstracts International 50/08-A: 2471.

GARRISON, W. L. (1968) "Connectivity of the interstate highway system," in B. J. L. Berry and D. F. Marble (eds.) Spatial Analysis: A Reader in Statistical Geography. Englewood Cliffs, NJ: Prentice-Hall.

GELFAND, A. E. (1969) Seriation of Multivariate Observations Through Similarities (Technical Report TR-146). Stanford, CA: Stanford University, Department of Statistics.

GELFAND, A. E. (1971) Rapid Seriation Methods With Applications (Technical Report TR-179). Stanford, CA: Stanford University, Department of Statistics.

GeoForum (1991) "NY county handles redistricting." Vol. 7(1): 3, 5.

GOODCHILD, M., and GOPAL, S. (1989) The Accuracy of Spatial Databases. London: Taylor & Francis.

GREEN, R. (1991) "Army rushes upgraded map system to Gulf." Government Computer News (February 18): 3.

GREIG-SMITH, P. (1952) "The use of random and contiguous quadrats in the study of the structure of plant communities." Annals of Botany (London) 16: 293-316.

GRIFFITH, D. A., and AMRHEIN, C. G. (1991) Statistical Analysis for Geographers. Englewood Cliffs, NJ: Prentice-Hall.

HÄGERSTRAND, T. (1968) "A Monte Carlo approach to diffusion," pp. 368-384 in B. J. L. Berry and D. F. Marble (eds.) Spatial Analysis: A Reader in Statistical Geography. Englewood Cliffs, NJ: Prentice-Hall.

HAGGETT, P. (1968) "Regional and local components in the distribution of forested areas in southeast Brazil: A multivariate approach," pp. 313-325 in B. J. L. Berry and D. F. Marble (ed.) Spatial Analysis: A Reader in Statistical Geography. Englewood Cliffs, NJ: Prentice-Hall.

HARBAUGH, J. W., and PRESTON, F. W. (1968) "Fourier series analysis in geology," pp. 218-238 in B. J. L. Berry and D. F. Marble (eds.) Spatial Analysis: A Reader in Statistical Geography. Englewood Cliffs, NJ: Prentice-Hall.

HATCH, J. W., MICHELS, J. W., STEVENSON, C. M., SCHEETZ, B. E., and GEIDEL, R. A. (1990) "Hopewell obsidian studies: Behavioral implications of recent sourcing and dating research." American Antiquity 55(3): 461-480.

HAWRYLYSHYN, O. (1977) "Yugoslav development and rural-urban migration: The evidence of the 1961 census," pp. 329-345 in A. A. Brown and E. Neuberger (eds.) Internal Migration: A Comparative Perspective. New York: Academic Press.

HILLIER, B. (1989) "The architecture of the urban object." Ekistics: The Problems and Science of Human Settlements 56(334): 5-17.

HINZE, K. E. (1989) "Reconciling data from different geographic databases." Social Science Computer Review 7(3): 285-295.

HOLE, F., and SHAW, M. (1967) "Computer analysis of chronological seriation." Rice University Studies 53(3): 1-166.

HOLMES, N. (1984) Designer's Guide to Creative Charts and Diagrams. New York: Watson-Guptil.

JANKOWSKI, P., and NYERGES, T. (1989) "Design considerations for MsPKBS—Map Projection Knowledge-Based System." American Cartographer 16(2): 85-95.

JENKS, G. F. (1963) "Generalization in statistical mapping." Annals of the Association of American Geographers 53: 15-26.

JENKS, G. F. (1975) "The evaluation and prediction of visual clustering in maps symbolized with proportional circles," pp. 311-327 in J. C. Davis and M. J. McCullagh (eds.) Display and Analysis of Spatial Data. New York: John Wiley.

JENKS, G. F. (1977) Optimal Data Classification for Choropleth Maps (Occasional Paper 2). Lawrence: University of Kansas, Department of Geography.

JENKS, G. F., and KNOS, D. S. (1961) "The use of shading patterns in graded series." Annals of the Association of American Geographers 51: 316-334.

JOHNSON, G. O. (1987) "Toward an emergency preparedness planning and operations system." URISA 1987 2: 171-183.

KENKEL, N. C., HOSKINS, J. A., and HOSKINS, W. D. (1989) "Edge effects in the use of area polygons to study competition." Ecology 70(1): 272-274.

KLOSTERMAN, R. E. (1988) "The literature of computers in planning," pp. 9-14 in R. E. Klosterman (ed.) A Planner's Review of PC Software and Technology (Planning Advisory Report 414/415). Chicago: American Planning Association.

KLOSTERMAN, R. E. (1989) Community Analysis and Planning Programs User Guide. Akron, OH: University of Akron, Center for Urban Studies.

KLOSTERMAN, R. E. (1990) "Microcomputers in urban and regional planning: Lessons from the past, directions for the future." Computers, Environment, and Urban Systems 14(3): 177-185.

KUMMLER, M. P., and GROOP, R. E. (1990) "Continuous-tone mapping of smooth surfaces." Cartography and Geographic Information Systems 17(4): 279-289.

LANGRAN, G. (1990) "Tracing temporal information in an automated nautical charting system." Cartography and Geographic Information Systems 17(4): 291-299.

LARSON, D. O., and MICHAELSEN, J. (1990) "Impacts of climatic variability and population growth on Virgin Branch Anasazi cultural developments." American Antiquity 55(2): 227-250.

LAVIN, S., and ARCHER, J. C. (1984) "Computer-produced unclassed bivariate choropleth maps." American Cartographer 11(1): 49-57.

LEE, J., and DOUGLASS, J. M. (1988) "Utilizing geographic information systems to assist in a municipality's effort to preserve clean water." URISA 1988 2: 88-96.

LEUNG, Y. (1988) Spatial Analysis and Planning Under Imprecision. New York: North-Holland.

MACKAY, J. R. (1949) "Dotting the dot map." Surveying and Mapping 9(1): 3-10.

MACKAY, J. R. (1968) "The interactance hypothesis and boundaries in Canada: A preliminary study," pp. 122-129 in B. J. L. Berry and D. F. Marble (eds.) Spatial Analysis: A Reader in Statistical Geography. Englewood Cliffs, NJ: Prentice-Hall.

MAK, K., and COULSON, M. R. C. (1991) "Map-user response to computer-generated choropleth maps: Comparative experiments in classification and symbolization." Cartography and Geographic Information Systems 18(2): 109-124.

MALING, D. H. (1973) Coordinate Systems and Map Projections. London: George Philip.

MALTZ, M. D., GORDON, A. C., and FRIEDMAN, W. (1991) Mapping Crime in Its Community Setting: Event Geography Analysis. New York: Springer-Verlag.

MANDELL, R. (1991). "Global mapping/geographical reference software for the political and social sciences." Social Science Computer Review 9(4): 558-574.

MARX, R. W. (ed.) (1990) The Census Bureau's TIGER System (special issue). Cartography and Geographic Information Systems 17(1).

MATHER, P. M. (1991) Computer Applications in Geography. New York: John Wiley.

MATSON, J. (1985) "Applying the SYMAP algorithm for surface compatibility and comparative analysis of areal data." American Cartographer 12(2): 114-122.

MATTHEWS, S. A. (1990) "Epidemiology using a GIS: The need for caution." Computers, Environment, and Urban Systems 14(3): 213-221.

McCULLOUGH, M. F. (1991) "Democratic questions for the computer age." Computers in Human Services 8(1): 9-18.

McDONNELL, P. W., Jr. (1979) Introduction to Map Projections. New York: Marcel Dekker.

McGRANAGHAN, M. (1989) "Ordering choropleth map symbols: The effect of background." American Cartographer 16(2): 279-285.

MEILACH, D. Z. (1990) Dynamics of Presentation Graphics (2nd ed.). Homewood, IL: Dow Jones-Irwin.

MILLER, J. C., and HONSAKER, J. L. (1983) "Visual versus computerized seriation: The implications for automated map generalization," pp. 277-287 in B. S. Wellar (ed.) Proceedings of the 6th International Symposium on Automated Cartography, Vol. 2: Automated Cartography—International Perspectives on Achievements and Challenges. Edmonton: University of Alberta, Department of Geography.

MOELLERING, H. (ed.) (1991a) Analytical Cartography (symposium issue). Cartography and Geographic Information Systems 18(1): 1-78.

MOELLERING, H. (1991b) "Whither analytic cartography?" Cartography and Geographic Information Systems 18(1): 7-9.

MONMONIER, M. S. (1982) Computer-Assisted Cartography: Principles and Prospects. Englewood Cliffs, NJ: Prentice-Hall.

MONMONIER, M. S. (1991) How to Lie With Maps. Chicago: University of Chicago Press.

MORAN, P. A. P. (1950) "Notes on continuous stochastic phenomena." Biometrika 37: 17-23.

NEWCOMER, J. A., and SZAJGIN, J. (1984) "Accumulation of thematic map errors in digital overlay analysis." American Cartographer 11(1): 58-62.

NYERGES, T. L. (1991) "Analytical map use." Cartography and Geographic Information Systems 18(1): 11-22.

NYERGES, T. L., and JANKOWSKI, P. (1989) "A knowledge base for map projection selection." American Cartographer 16(1): 29-38.

O'KELLY, M. E., and MILLER, H. J. (1989) "A synthesis of some market area delimitation models." Growth and Change 20(3): 14-33.

OMURA, G. (1989) Mastering AutoCAD (3rd ed.). Alameda, CA: Sybex.

PARENT, P., and CHURCH, R. (1989) "Evolution of geographic information systems as decision making tools," pp. 9-18 in W. J. Ripple (ed.) Fundamentals of Geographic Information Systems: A Compendium. Bethesda, MD: American Society for Photogrammetry and Remote Sensing and the American Congress on Surveying and Mapping.

PASLAWSKI, J. (1984) "In search of a general idea of class selection for choropleth maps." International Yearbook of Cartography 24: 159-169.

PASSARIS, C. (1989) "Immigration and the evolution of economic theory." International Migration 27(4): 525-542.

PETERSON, M. P. (1979) "An evaluation of unclassed cross-line choropleth mapping." American Cartographer 6: 21-37.

PROVIN, R. W. (1977) "The perception of numerousness on dot maps." American Cartographer 4: 111-125.

RAISZ, E. (1935) "Rectangular statistical cartograms of the world." Journal of Geography 35: 8-10.

RAVENSTEIN, E. G. (1976) The Laws of Migration. New York: Arno. (Original work published in two parts, 1885 and 1889)

RICE, G. H. (1990) "Teaching students to become discriminating map users." Social Education 54(6): 393-397.

RICHARDSON, P., and ADLER, R. K. (1972) Map Projections. Amsterdam: North-Holland.

RIPPLE, W. J. (ed.) (1989) Fundamentals of Geographic Information Systems: A Compendium. Bethesda, MD: American Society for Photogrammetry and Remote Sensing and the American Congress on Surveying and Mapping.

ROBB, D. W. (1990) "Netting crooks easier with micro center guidance." Government Computer News (February 5): 15.

ROBERTSON, B. (1988) How to Draw Charts and Diagrams. Cincinnati, OH: North Light.

ROBINSON, A. H., LINDBERG, J. B., and BRINKMAN, L. W. (1968) "A correlation and regression analysis applied to rural farm population densities in the Great Plains," pp. 290-300 in B. J. L. Berry and D. F. Marble (ed.) Spatial Analysis: A Reader in Statistical Geography. Englewood Cliffs, NJ: Prentice-Hall.

ROBINSON, A. H., SALE, R. D., MORRISON, J. L., and MUEHRCKE, P. C. (1984) Elements of Cartography (5th ed.). New York: John Wiley.

ROESSAL, J. W. VAN (1989) "An algorithm for locating candidate labeling boxes within a polygon." American Cartographer 16(3): 201-209.

ROGERS, A. (1974) Statistical Analysis of Spatial Dispersion: The Quadrat Method. London: Pion.

ROOTMAN, P. J. (1988) "Blanke migrasie na Port Elizabeth, 1900-1979" [White migration to Port Elizabeth, 1900-1979]. South African Geographer 16(1-2): 68-80.

ROSCH, W. L. (1990) "Survivors: Desktop plotters face the competition." PC Magazine (March 27): 134-168.

SAMET, H. (1990) The Design and Analysis of Spatial Data Structures. Reading, MA: Addison-Wesley.

SAUNDERS, M. N. K. (1983) The Growth of Nineteenth Century Barrow-in-Furness: Some Insights into Current Migration Theory (Discussion Papers in Geography 25). Salford, England: University of Salford.

SCHROEDER, E. (1991) "MapInfo readies real-time vehicle tracking system." PC Week (November 4): 30.

SELKIRK, K. (1982) Pattern and Place: An Introduction to the Mathematics of Geography. New York: Cambridge University Press.

SHEPARD, D. (1968) A Two-Dimensional Interpolation Function for Computer Mapping of Irregularly Spaced Data (Geography and the Property of Surfaces, Paper 15). Cambridge, MA: Harvard Center for Environmental Designs.

SHERYAEV, E. E. (1977) Computers and the Representation of Geographical Data. New York: John Wiley.

SHIMBEL, A. (1953) "Structural parameters of communication networks." Bulletin of Mathematical Biophysics 15: 501-507.

SMITH, R. M. (1986) "Comparing traditional methods for selecting class intervals on choropleth maps." Professional Geographer 38(1): 62-67.

SNYDER, J. P. (1987) Map Projections: A Working Manual (U.S. Geological Survey Professional Paper 1395). Washington, DC: Government Printing Office.

SNYDER, J. P., and STEWARD, H. (eds.) (1988) Bibliography of Map Projections (U.S. Geological Survey Bulletin 1856). Denver: U.S. Geological Survey, Books and Open-File Reports Sections.

SOUTHALL, H., and OLIVER, E. (1990) "Drawing maps with a computer . . . or without?" History and Computing 2(2): 146-154.

SRINIVASAN, P. (1990) "Computational geometric methods in volumetric intersection for 3D reconstruction." Ph.D. dissertation, University of California, Santa Barbara.

STEFANOVIC, P., and DRUMMOND, J. (1989) "Selection and evaluation of computer-assisted mapping and geo information systems," pp. 215-220 in W. J. Ripple (ed.) Fundamentals of Geographic Information Systems: A Compendium. Bethesda, MD: American Society for Photogrammetry and Remote Sensing and the American Congress on Surveying and Mapping.

STEWART, J. Q., and WARNTZ, W. (1968) "Physics of population distribution," pp. 130-146 in B. J. L. Berry and D. F. Marble (eds.) Spatial Analysis: A Reader in Statistical Geography. Englewood Cliffs, NJ: Prentice-Hall.

SUTTON, J. (1988) Lotus Focus on Graphics (5 vols.). Cambridge, MA: Lotus Development Corporation.

TAFT, D. K. (1991) "VA's GIS analyzes future health facility options." Government Computer News (April 1): 17.

TAYLOR, C. L. (1986) "A rectangular tessellation with computational and database advantages," pp. 391-402 in B. Diaz and S. Bell (eds.) Spatial Data Processing Using Tesseral Methods. Newbury, U.K.: Digital Research Ltd., Oxford House, for the NERC Unit for Thematic Information Systems, University of Reading.

THOMAS, E. N. (1968) "Maps of residuals from regression," pp. 326-352 in B. J. L. Berry and D. F. Marble (eds.) Spatial Analysis: A Reader in Statistical Geography. Englewood Cliffs, NJ: Prentice-Hall.

THOMAS, R. M. (1989) Advanced Techniques in AutoCAD (2nd ed.). Alameda, CA: Sybex.

TOBLER, W. R. (1961) "Map transformations of geographic space." Ph.D. dissertation, University of Washington, Seattle.

TOBLER, W. R. (1968) "Geographic area and map projections," pp. 78-90 in B. J. L. Berry and D. F. Marble (eds.) Spatial Analysis: A Reader in Statistical Geography. Englewood Cliffs, NJ: Prentice-Hall.

Tomlinson Associates, Ltd. (1989) "Current and potential uses of geographical information systems: The North American experience," pp. 167-182 in W. J. Ripple (ed.) Fundamentals of Geographic Information Systems: A Compendium. Bethesda, MD: American Society for Photogrammetry and Remote Sensing and the American Congress on Surveying and Mapping.

TUFTE, E. R. (1983) The Visual Display of Quantitative Information. Cheshire, CT: Graphics.

U.S. Bureau of the Census (1979) Census Geography (Data Access Description 22). Washington, DC: Government Printing Office.

U.S. General Accounting Office (1991) Geographic Information Systems: Information on Federal Use and Coordination (Report GAO/IMTEC-91-72FS, September 27). Washington, DC: Government Printing Office.

WAREING, J. (1981) "Migration to London and transatlantic emigration of indentured servants, 1683-1775." Journal of Historical Geography 7(4): 356-378.

WARNECKE, L. (1990) "Geographic information systems: Team tries to find common ground for spatial data." Government Computer News (November 26): 45-47.

WEISBURD, D., MAHER, L. S., and SHERMAN, L. W. (1989) "Contrasting crime general and crime specific theory: The case of hot spots of crime." Presented at the annual meeting of the American Sociological Association, San Francisco.

WILDGEN, J. K. (1989) "Gerrymanders and gerrygons: Microcomputer-assisted spatial analytic approaches to vote dilution detection." Social Science Computer Review 7(2): 147-160.

WILLIAMS, R. E. (1987) "Selling a geographical information system to government policy makers." URISA 1987 3: 150-156.

WILSON, A. G., and KIRKBY, M. J. (1980) Mathematics for Geographers and Planners (2nd ed.). New York: Oxford University Press.

WITSCHEY, W. R. T. (1989) "An architectural seriation of the pre-Hispanic structures at Muyil, Quintana Roo, Mexico." Master's Abstracts 28/04: 512.

WONG, S. T. (1968) "A multivariate statistical model for predicting mean annual flood in New England," pp. 353-367 in B. J. L. Berry and D. F. Marble (eds.) Spatial Analysis: A Reader in Statistical Geography. Englewood Cliffs, NJ: Prentice-Hall.

ZELAZNY, G. (1985) Say It With Charts: The Executive's Guide to Successful Presentations. Homewood, IL: Dow Jones-Irwin.

ABOUT THE AUTHORS

G. DAVID GARSON is Professor of Political Science and Public Administration at North Carolina State University. He is editor of the *Social Science Computer Review*, published by Duke University Press, and is author or editor of a dozen books and monographs on research methods, public administration, and American politics, including *Advances in Social Science and Computers* (JAI Press, Vol. 1, 1990; Vol. 2, 1991) and *Computers in Public Employee Relations* (International Personnel Management Association, 1988). He founded National Collegiate Software, now part of William C. Brown, Publishers. He is also Associate Dean for Planning and Management in the College of Humanities and Social Sciences at NCSU, in which capacity he oversees four computer laboratories in economics, social science, humanities, and foreign languages. He is a graduate of Princeton and Harvard Universities.

ROBERT S. BIGGS is Director of Community Development and Planning for the town of Wendell, North Carolina. He is completing his master's degree in the Public Administration Program at North Carolina State University and is scheduled for graduation in spring 1992.

Quantitative Applications in the Social Sciences

A SAGE UNIVERSITY PAPER SERIES

$10.95 each

To order, please use order form on the next page.

Quantitative Applications in the Social Sciences

A SAGE UNIVERSITY PAPER SERIES

$10.95 each

Place
Stamp
here

SAGE PUBLICATIONS, INC.
P.O. BOX 5084
THOUSAND OAKS, CALIFORNIA 91359-9924